Environment
and Learning

Environment and Learning:
The Prior Issues

Charles R. Reid

Rutherford · Madison · Teaneck
Fairleigh Dickinson University Press
London: Associated University Presses

Associated University Presses, Inc.
Cranbury, New Jersey 08512

Associated University Presses
Magdalen House
136-148 Tooley Street
London SE1 2TT, England

Library of Congress Cataloging in Publication Data

Reid, Charles R   1926 —
    Environment and learning.

    Bibliography: p.
    Includes index.
    1. Educational sociology. 2. School environment.
    3. Human ecology — Study and teaching. I. Title.
LC191.R44   370.19'3   75-36526
ISBN 0-8386-1711-5

PRINTED IN THE UNITED STATES OF AMERICA

Contents

Preface

Philosophy of education is intrinsically a difficult subject. In its purely theoretical stage it intimidates by its demand for abstraction and synthesis. Yet one faces an even more perplexing challenge if he claims the right to translate a philosophy into practice, especially in a time of alternating, often inexplicable, clashing restraints and freedoms in the existing systems of formal education. When a critic such as myself suggests a new look at reality, calling for a contemporary philosophy of education based on what he postulates are the needs of contemporary (and future) society, his views may rightfully seem suspect. The outlook on life that is asked for is judged too demanding, too simplistic, or — even more damning -- too conceited in its globalism. Yet his book, like any other, has its goal, and the reader is asked to accept an invitation to travel the road that hopefully leads to that goal, to share at least some part of the writer's vision, a new vision in certain respects but in others an extremely old one — the vision of man living in harmony with his surroundings.

Environment as a subject of interest and study has seemed to burst upon the public mind almost unheralded, arriving suddenly in a cloud of radical jingoism. But as we stop to reflect, we may concede that the issue has been with us for a very long time. It has exercised such significantly original minds as those of the Greek humanist philosophers, the medieval scholastics, and the utopian writers from More to Marx. Today, with the mixed burdens and blessings of scientific knowledge, man faces his natural and social habitat — the same habitat that his ancestors knew, albeit knew far less well in the sense of comprehending its limitations — with new weapons as well as new fears. He aches with a desire to explore the still-virgin depths of his own psyche in an expanding effort to achieve greater oneness with the universe. He has already traveled a significant distance, asserting terrible dominion both over other living creatures and over the cold outer reaches of the cosmos. But still he must struggle with himself; he must still seek the key to his own behavior. This is a search as difficult as that for the universal principle itself, yet to such a search the present volume addresses itself.

In any individual view of an environment, certain constants are present. One tends to think of a milieu inhabited by living creatures as made up of a series of complex *processes*. These in turn require a fixed minimum of *resources* as the basis of their physical continuation. The processes are termed the biotic factors in plant or animal existence (e.g., food chains, biogeochemical cycles, succession, etc.) and the resources are termed abiotic factors (i.e., soil, water, light, etc.). While science deals in these terms of reference almost exclusively, the philosopher naturally finds them inadequate, most immediately on psychological grounds. By preserving the fiction of the "uninvolved" observer, however necessary in the cause of pure science, the essential psychological entity of the *self* in the interaction of living organisms may be lost sight of. To the environmental thinker this is a fundamental error.

Wherever coping behavior or adjustmental effort by any organism occurs, a milieu-affecting mechanism has been at work. Psychological reaction to the organism's surroundings has added another dimension to the net total of interactions within that environment. When reaction is also behaviorally forceful enough, it disturbs the total environmental balance. Readjustments must then take place throughout the system, which under certain circumstances can be a socially traumatic experience.

One does not have to seek far for evidences of this. Man's behavior in the industrial age up to the present gives a clear-cut example of such an upset of system-wide balance. We humans have, for our own purposes, overturned or destroyed vital links in natural food chains, have altered important natural patterns of succession, and have broken down biogeochemical cycles with callous disregard for what these actions might mean in the maintenance of an overall balance of life on this planet. We have abused our soils, polluted our water, and cast up a veil of smog to filter sunlight, in each case the better to insure our temporary bodily comforts and our eventual bodily degradation. What is important to note in this regard is that these ill effects have not come about solely through man's unregulatable impulsive behavior or inability to conceive of and accept alternatives, but have apparently been approved as part of a presumably larger plan. They have come about because all too often they were a necessary write-off in a commercial scheme directed toward ends held to be of superior importance. It is impossible to avoid the assumption that man has been, and continues to be, *cognitively* involved in the negation, as well as the assertion, of his alliance to nature. It follows that there is no more proper study for these times than that of the human mind at its work of adjusting man's relations with his life-sustaining environment.

Such a study should begin with a clear understanding of the basic concepts being dealt with. In particular, the terms *ecological* and *environmental* tend to become confused. Ecology, the study of interrelationships among living organisms and between such organisms and their milieu, is correctly viewed as a science that aims to elicit valid interpretations of observable events, or chains of events, in natural settings. But to the ecologist, man is only one organism among the many functioning in a complex environment. The emphasis on man's *unique* capability for affecting any earthly environment may or may not be stressed. The study called human ecology constitutes, it is true, one effort to redress the balance, but this approach focuses more particularly on the "how" of the process rather than the "why" or "to what end?"

In this volume a distinct and continuous emphasis *is* placed on man's behavior as a powerful but shifting and unpredictable force in terrestrial affairs. The need for this emphasis seems clear. Man throughout history has tended to view the universe from his own particularist vantage point, all too often that of the unthinking exploiter. Man has never relaxed without first having secured his own comforts and perquisites, and this has so much colored his outlook that by self-conditioning he tends to see nature solely in "it-against-me" terms. But he differs from all other organisms in the ability to engage in reflection and planning as a means of using for his own purposes whatever exists apart from himself. Human history appears in one sense as one undivided and protracted struggle to attain security and to make man the dominant form of planetary life. The wisdom of this point of view seems now open to question, and any inquiry designed to explore alternative positions becomes a matter of more than passing importance. To such an inquiry this book is devoted.

The term *environment*, rather than *ecology*, dominates the discussions that constitute this volume, for the obvious reason that it best conveys the idea of *man's* behaving and reacting against the field of forces that nature provides — the guiding theme of all that follows. The units that make up this collection of thoughts are termed chapters for the sake of convenience rather than to indicate any necessary order. They are better seen as so many variations upon a theme — that of man's behavior in his environment; and, as with the variations on a theme required by the schools of European classical music, the author's intention is to provide in each succeeding departure from the basic *tema* some new glimpse of the significance of the fixed germinal motif.

The chapters that follow are independent, yet so organized that they build something of a cumulative argument for a more adaptive education in an evolving modern society. The introductory chapter explains my philosophic point of view. Chapter 2 is expository and informational, a brief view of basic issues in environmental education. Chapter 3 opens the Pandora's box of adult learning and behavior and, following a general analysis of the social basis for learning, suggests a new direction in mass adult education for the coming environmental age. The next three chapters consider formal education in light of the environmental hypothesis. Chapter 4 examines the old opposition between general and specialized learning, against a background of projected environmental-era needs. Chapter 5 considers the role of traditional learning and its liabilities for a society entering an epoch of radically swift social change. Chapter 6 seeks, through an examination of the nature-nurture controversy in an environmental context, to pave the way for a plan of institutional synthesis, a model of the new "environmental" school for youth from twelve to twenty. Chapter 7 retutns to the philosophic thread of the Introduction, making an attempt to focus more clearly on reasons, pragmatic and axiological, for the deliberate cultivation of environmental behavior through a program of experience both socially and personally developmental.

In much of this book I have seen my task as not so much one of breaking entirely new ground as of bringing together, to the extent possible, those fragments of discrete thought which seem to require integration in the process of facing up squarely to the environmental predicament — a predicament that man has all too slowly come to realize is uniquely his to solve. This task requires a certain eclecticism of approach, or at least a willingness to sift various concepts and views of reality (especially from contemporary social science). But the tendency to make the whole study no more than a "survey" of different schools of thought has been resisted.

Each separate essay consists of an interpretation of a major topic — the statement, elaboration, and defense of one point of view of that topic, as opposed to a comparative discussion of a number of points of view, to all of which the writer might show an equal indifference. This permits the reader to form his own counterarguments or to develop counter-theories by himself, rather than having to struggle through textbook explications laid before him in a manner of a lecture course, one following another in an inexorable sequence so carefully plotted that few readers feel called upon to use their own mental resources in responding critically to the author's point of view. There is in all this one overriding purpose: to stimulate thinking, and ultimately action, on new modes of human adaptation to a finite universe, and to create a more suitable climate for such adaptation at a time when that universe is physically shrinking and socially expanding far too swiftly for human safety or comfort.

Acknowledgments

To my former colleagues at Iowa Wesleyan College — Donald Ziegler, Joseph Mauck, and Vincent Mahoney — I give thanks for their interest and encouragement during the period of this book's gestation. To Dr. Harry Colfer, of San Francisco and Palm Springs, I owe also a debt for his encouragement and support in my writing efforts over many years. To Julien Yoseloff of A. S. Barnes and Associated University Presses and to the editorial board of Fairleigh Dickinson University Press I express my gratitude for their long-term concern over the many problems involved in book publication as well as for their continuing belief in both the value of the subject of this volume and its relevance for today's reader. Also I would thank Dr. Dale Baughman and his staff at Indiana State University for their willingness to give initial publication to my article "Notes on Environmental Education," the synoptic statement of the basis of the further development of ideas fully elaborated in this book.

To the reader of this volume, also, thanks should be given for his curiosity, his endurance, his concern for humanity's welfare, and his openness to new, unvarnished, or even highly disturbing suggestions or trains of thought. If the effort that this volume represents on the writer's part is matched by a corresponding involvement on the average reader's part,

13

neither will come away from the encounter any the worse. No one has more to gain from an increase in knowledge of our environmental predicament than the aware human being who honestly intends to live adaptively with his surroundings. I hope that it may serve as a model for futute mental activity by those who seek a state of awareness with knowledge. Environments create their own laws; our struggle must be to learn those laws and live with them to the best of our ability, whatever the emotional cost and expenditure of moral or physical effort.

Appreciation is expressed to Indiana State University, publisher of CONTEMPORARY EDUCATION, in the pages of which first appeared my "Notes on Environmental Education," reprinted here with minor alteration as chapter 2 (The Basis of Environmental Education), for permission to reproduce that material as an integral part of the present publication. "Notes on Environmental Education" was published in CONTEMPORARY EDUCATION, 46, no. 2 (Winter 1975): 95-99.

Appreciation is also due the firm of Routledge and Kegan Paul, London, publishers of Jean Piaget and associates, *The Moral Judgment of the Child* (1932), from which extensive quotation is made in chapter 5 of the present volume, and the Free Press (Glencoe, Ill.) for American rights.

Environment and Learning

1

Introduction: Why Study the Linkage of Environment and Learning?

In the discussions that constitute this volume, the emphasis is on an integration of behavior, individual and group, along lines that accord with an environmental ethic yet also take into account less-than-ideal social and psychological, or economic, imperatives. An effort has been made to develop something like a balanced *human* frame of reference for the entire environmental question. Certain assumptions underlie the series of essays, important among which are: that learning in some measure governs behavior; that mass human behavior, in turn, is governed in some degree, however rough, by mass learning; that man's idiosyncratic ways of viewing nature constitute an important prior condition in determining modes of environmental change; and, finally, that change

17

of any kind can at best be minimally (although not, perhaps, insignificantly) directed.

In this consideration of the scope of concern for the mechanics and outcomes of behavior that affect both physical and mental environments, it should be understood that the learning and behavior brought into question are looked on as worldwide, and are not limited geographically to any one area. Further, no *a priori lack* of connection is posited between human behavior and prior learning situations, simple or complex. The cynic shallowly suggests that an examination of some particular phenomenon of childhood thinking "has really no bearing on our stopping the trans-Alaskan pipeline" or "does nothing to save us from those who would revive the SST (Supersonic Transport)." The rebuttal lies in the adage favored by many environmentalists of the militant school: we must always try to see and understand the *interconnectedness* of all things.

Environmental learning, if it is to fulfill the needs of contemporary and future man, must involve more than just the invocation of some modernized version of old pantheistic doctrine, which found a god in every leaf and pebble. The theme of "man the measure of all things" similarly leaves much to be desired; certainly it falls short, and seriously so, to the degree that it asserts the "natural" claim of man to superiority over the rest of nature. Yet establishing a new touchstone for an environmental conscience is no easy labor. Frontal attacks on human vanity or appetite only serve to make us question the intent of the attacker, rather than focusing attention on the problem of why the behavior of humanity is what it is.

Futurism has not become by accident a major preoccupation of leading contemporary scholars. In its own restricted sphere this book too concerns the world of tomorrow. It is involved with the problems of change as they relate to man's learning, for his ability to learn and grow will determine in high degree his effectiveness in responding to change. My question can be simply put: to what degree can the learning thrust be directed to further environmentally valid (rather than inappropriate) human behavior?

Thought about, and action on behalf of the environment, are evolving reactions of a complex organism, man, to a complex world. Human society may itself prove the most serious stumbling block to the required new forms of environmental accomodation in which case man will then contrive to evolve to a more successful mode of social existence. So too, if man finds his body (say, for example, the nervous system, perhaps the most endangered of his biological subsystems under the strains of modern urban life) inadequate to the task of adaptation, the body itself will evolve to a new and more biologically effective state of being. But such developments are time-consuming, and man — modern man more than any of his forebears in history and prehistory — finds time the most serious of all his enemies, a baffling, superior antagonist.

Time glides by at the organismic or social levels as essentially a neutral force, a stream in which the business of existence must flow, without being subject to evaluation. Time is a problem for the only entity in creation capable of seeing it as such — the aspiring mind. Man finds to his irritation that he can no more hurry nature than he can with impunity abuse it. His body and his society, both moved by impulses beyond his own direct control, can evolve to higher adaptive stages only in a natural way. This being so, and since man is fixated on maximizing time for his own purposes, there is left only his own mind as a locus for change: he can expand his experience mentally, since other avenues of approach make change too slow, too imperceptible in development, to afford him the satisfactions he seeks.

But this restriction itself has possible beneficial spin-off effects. If man can recognize the futility of forever seeking to harness nature for his own exclusive purposes and instead can aim to pursue the far-from-finished task of exploring his own inner resources, the results could signal a new era in the relationship between man and nature. Indeed, the two factors may be seen as twin and inseparable elements in the universal human effort towards perfection. It was the belief of the late Lecomte du Noüy that in the later stages of man's tenure on earth only mental evolution would remain as a possible path of further development for the species, a mental evolution stressing moral growth and capacity above all else.[1] The emergence of environment as a fit theme for man's universal striving marks at long last a field in which this kind of cosmic view of human possibilities can be studied.

There are also other points of view and other contributory figures. In seeing the universe as a vast, chaotic, essentially alien milieu for man, Nietzsche performed a service for philosophy and education in the modern industrial world. He provided us with a salutary rejoinder to the belief of the Enlightenment that *all* parameters of existence could be fixed within a rationalist framework. The lesson of this teaching for our time is that the problem of man versus his environment will not be solved by rigid application of rationalist doctrines now, any more than the social problems of eighteenth-century France could be solved by Jacobin idealist dialectics. Nevertheless, the wholesale abandonment of the point of view of rational science as developed in such difficult, often pitifully slow stages since the beginnings of technology, with its attendant rationalization of social life to carry forward the purposes of industrial growth, cannot be entertained without at the same time breaking with the whole continuity of human social evolution through history — a price too high to pay, even for the extremists who see it as the only way out of our environmental dilemma.

It is necessary, whether we like it or not, to seek a harmonious coexistence of man with nature. In some part the attainment of such proper coexistence involves man's beliefs and practices in the effort to realize himself fully. Perhaps, as Nietzsche held in *The Use and Abuse of History*, the pendulum that swung away from art and religion and toward science in the earlier industrial era must be clearly and consciously reversed and new monuments of beauty and faith be fashioned from mankind's experience if the species is to retain any serious regard for itself as a factor in the functioning universe.[2] Yet technology, the fruit of a science dearly purchased and a bulwark against so many of nature's own blind injustices, cannot be viewed as merely some disagreeable excrescence invented by a few self-seeking scions of the industrial system to impede the general development of the race. It is, as a fact of modern life, the one most necessary prerequisite to that level of existence which permits all the more refined expressions of human sensibility. Man cannot do without technology in a majority of its forms, and the question now becomes one of deciding which forms of technology are the best fitted for inclusion in the equation of man-with-nature, as against the old one of man-against-nature.

If the atomistic specialization of thought and labor that industrialized humankind has accepted as necessary to technological/social progress is to be balanced by a more humane group-consciousness, why should not environment become the leading motif around which such consciousness can develop? Environment, if broadly enough defined, provides a focal point that all the race can accept in the universal rush for self-fulfillment; it is a common interest that can be shared and have more meaning for individuals than the crumbing values of pursuits (e.g., upward social mobility) that have proved to be of less than universal significance.

But any movement to "environmentalize" man's thinking and behavior may pose new dangers, possibly more destructive than what it would supplant. If the environmental campaign, so roughly begun, ends by becoming only another secular religion followed by a small group of articulate adherents, it will have fallen far short of its potential. As a religion or crusade, its success will likely prove wholly transitory and ineffectual. As the agent of furthering genuinely *human* purposes in a universe of changing shapes and meanings, however, environment holds the promise of unifying world society, even as it has already served to unify

a small group of advanced thinkers, along with their alert
followers among the world's intelligentsia.

   In this regard it is also a matter of some importance to
accept that now, more than ever before in history, education
does not begin or end at the schoolhouse door. When the
overall organization of social life has such a level of complexity as at present, all institutions of society become radically
interdependent, and some rather more than others. As
Jencks has recently shown in an analysis of family factors as
they affect children's "equality of educational opportunity,"
the school itself lacks any really natural capability for enforcing social reform or acting as an equalizer.[3] People consistently expect schools to perform wonders, but the school
seems to be one of those institutions peculiarly incapable of
bringing about social miracles.
   Much of this book is concerned with the phenomenon
of learning as it operates in the whole society and not in the
formal scholastic setting alone. In the sense of "environmental" learning conveyed in what follows, the organism
that achieves significant learning does so by developing
an ever-expanding sensitivity to the self and its surroundings
in its chain of experience. History indicates that the world
will, as humankind "progresses," steadily invade the individual's private thoughts, challenging him — continually and
at rising levels of complexity — to integrate his behavior into
the swirl of the sociophysical universe. The learning in
question is both more necessary and more demanding than
any heretofore expected of man; it compels him to adapt —
to become among the fittest, or else fail to survive — by
optimizing all those still-latent, half-developed faculties for
further evolution (his own body, his cognitive capacity,
his affective capabilities) as he struggles to perceive and
react successfully to an environment more nearly universal
in its influence over him than any before known. Schools
have their part to play in this emerging process, but their

success will be limited to the degree that they are followers rather than leaders in the evolutionary social development of man. It is necessary to think of them as adjuncts, helpers, and valuable testing sites rather than as agents of social evolution *per se*, at least until a more dynamic role is assigned them.

The adaptive learning referred to, it should be understood also, is not to be confused with so-called adjustment learning of the kind generally associated (with pejorative connotation) with the Progressive or Experimentalist schools of educational theory. While learning to cope with conflict perceived in "they-against-me" terms does have a part to play only in the organism's physical survival, little is accomplished in terms of "environmental" learning when the individual is unable to progress beyond this stage. This is so because learning that accords with environmental needs goes much farther in the direction of integrating the person with his surroundings, and mitigates destructive forms of experience or at least preserves the learner from their harsher effects on personality and direction of growth. Environmental learning will optimize possibilities for individual fulfillment and build toward those behavior patterns which preserve rather than destroy self-worth and purpose, at the same time making adjustment the prerequisite element it must always in the philosophical sense be — namely, the basis for renewed capability of self-development, never merely an end in itself.

Some mention should be made of the "adjustment" theory as it applies in the environmental context to formal learning, inasmuch as social behavior is an important part of the educational process and is indeed usually considered one major goal of education. The child, as is so often remarked, cannot be expected to behave as a man. But the object of any education must in some degree be to modify behavior. Thus, out of the contrast of present inclination and future need a *trend* of behavior may be observed, and it is this that must be judged. Any presently noted "level of adjustment" is merely a sample from a limited context of behaviors.

This is tantamount to saying that the teacher who observes a child only in the formal educational setting has an insufficeint basis for considering behavior in that setting an end in itself, something to teach for directly and on which the student will (in all seriousness) be graded. Until the school curriculum is enlarged to admit a greater interplay of experiences by which the student can engage his potential for a participation symbolic of his full range of behavioral capability, he is being unfairly and, in the majority of cases, inaccurately judged. "Life adjustment" as represented by a teacher's rating of that small sample of behavior the student displays in class has, in short, no real significance. Adjustment to a formal educational milieu cannot be shown to relate in a meaningful way to what I have termed environmental learning and behavior.

The question of what can be done within a formal school setting to develop environmental learning and behavior will be taken up later, in several chapters, but a few words should be said here regarding one other element in formal education that is under reexamination in light of environmental concerns and the changing needs of contemporary man. This is the position and function of the various subjects studied in the ordinary school curriculum.

A prime problem with this curriculum is that the public understanding of environmental education credits only the physical sciences with any relevance to the attack on environmental problems, with the unfortunate result of freezing the *formal* study of such problems into the physical science portion of the existing curriculum when the generation of an entirely new curriculum was called for. Two results of this identification of environmental problems with the physical sciences alone are particularly noteworthy. First, an unsatisfactory basis for learning has been established among teachers and students, which could have a significant effect on the human aspect of environmental behavior. Second, with this approach the movement to environmentalize man's thinking is left in the hands of a minority leadership that lacks the openness and flexibility of response, as well as the initiative, to bring about lasting change.

Since what goes on in the schools, however little it may now serve to build into future gererations of citizens capacities to adapt to radically and swiftly shifting conditions of life, has some relation at all times to the adaptability of the total society, there must come about soon some remedy of the imbalance between physical science and all the other traditional subjects; if this does not occur as an offshoot of the process of "environmentalizing" the curriculum, it will be forced by that process. The likelihood is that as environmental points of view penetrate further and deeper into the collective consciousness of those who control the curricula of schools, the traditional parceling out of knowledge by way of the separate subjects and their pedagogues will have ceased to exist. Meanwhile, we face a need to bring to students an awareness of how environment relates to all existing disciplines.

> Our imaginations require feeding as well as our ventral organs. Thus environmental education should from the start involve every discipline, every coign of vantage of the educational establishment. There is simply no logical reason at all for environmental education to become the property of natural scientists alone.[4]

The whole issue of how the school succeeds or fails in its effort to integrate out-of-school learning with its own provision of formal learning experiences has a good deal to do with environmental learning.[5] The environmental approach implicitly requires such integration, but only under certain circumstances and with the clearest of mandates from the centers of authority that act to accept or reject broad school policy. In the chapters below that deal with learning in formal situations (chapters 4, 5, and 6) and elsewhere, suggestions are made that reflect my views on how the school and society may be made to merge in their effects on the learner's consciousness and on his decision-making.

School learning and the outside world's influences upon the student cannot easily be held apart. In today's turbulent climate of change and insecurity, no educator worthy of the name can avoid this charge: to provide an education that comes as close as possible to meeting the needs of an individual who perceives life more realistically, with more of a sense of entrangement and yet with more of a pervasive hope, than any of his forefathers; and to provide an education that gives that individual better equipment for coping with his fears and uncertainties yet does not coddle him or paint a false picture of his future — a future that he knows will be as full of conflict as of satisfactions.

The ineffective educator finds himself falling back on formulae as outdated in substance as they are in the language used to maintain them. Of what use is the approach that would preserve the age-old rationalization expressed by "This hurts me more than it does you"? While the human weakness implied in this *haut-en-bas* defense of behavior makes a good basis for the television joke, it becomes increasingly irrelevant and even harmful in the setting of formal education. The newer psychology of the classroom has involved the turning of a corner in human relations; the notion that something altogether beneficial can be done for another member of the species *in spite of his objections and failure to comprehend why* touches a raw nerve in the educational critic who has kept abreast of the times. With reason can accusations of paternalism, and of coercion without moral justification, be raised. But the conundrum posed by the continuing question "How to teach?" serves to remind us of the challenge faced by the professional educator as demands for accountability and relevance mount and society's relations with the formal institutions of education become more abrasive by the hour. We can also see better, perhaps, why learning is so hard to direct in a modern industrial society and why that learning which is of the greatest potential importance to the race — that which promotes flexibility in altering behavior patterns already in being — is the hardest learning of all to secure.

There appears to exist in the typical contemporary human being's view of himself in the universe an even more global, empirical justification for the study of environmental learning and behavior. One cannot speak of human learning today in solely an elitist context, that of a minority of fortunate citizens of a few fortunate countries blessed with the resources to develop formal education. There are below this level men in all stages of moral and mental development who are striving to survive in conditions of life becoming steadily more complex. Humanity, despite such inequalities, faces common problems that will remain unsolved or be resolved accordingly as men behave. But men are individuals and learn as individuals. Personally held values and beliefs regarding what paths to seek in the effort at self-realization emerge out of the experience of learning. What men learn, therefore, must seriously influence their behavior and, in so doing, affect their future chances of survival.

We are well aware of contemporary negative reactions to traditional formal education in an advanced society. With the spread of modern concepts of government, of economic and industrial development, and of mass society as a cybernated unit, these reactions threaten to become general throughout the industrial world. The element of manipulation in those situations involving informal learning (e.g., via the media, government, advertising) places a similar taint on experiences formerly considered "natural" or "necessary."

Any situation in which the learner reacts to all perceived stimuli with patent defiance creates complications for those concerned with engendering more idiosyncratic and adaptive behavior. Educationally speaking, a whole battery of rejective reactions will be drawn upon at will by persons exposed to contemporary learning stimuli, under both formal and informal circumstances; these include negativism, alienation, expressed hatred of experiences seen as artificially imposed,

and, in extreme cases, self-rejection in face of the challenge
of any serious learning.

The adult world is frequently viewed in psychological
terms as largely dominated by such factors. One is reminded
that the outcomes of such rejective efforts are all too closely
observable in any modern society. Adults behave with an
attitude of futility in major human undertakings and react
with a scarcely hidden disgust in those cases where they are
conscious of being manipulated, toward ends they cannot
ascertain sufficiently in advance or ends they feel are determined by others.

This formidable expression of adult estrangement is
adopted by today's teenager before he has developed so much
as a foothold in the realm of grown-up behavior, and it
poses serious questions for both the critic of society at large
and the purveyor of change in formal education. And both
the broader social questions and those specific to formal
education are germane to the work of a student of environmental learning. It would be a grave error to overstress the
larger society's capacity to resist meaningful behavioral
change and thereby to underemphasize the potential of
systems of formal education to expedite and smooth the
way for such change. What the school can do for society may
yet prove of more significance than many critics of formal
education currently care to admit; genuinely reciprocal
relations between institutions of formal education and the
broader society cannot exist without more effective operational definition of a balance in responsibilities, and toward
this theoretical point of balance, then, mankind must work.

A final word is apropos regarding the terms *environment*
and *environmentalism*. The conception of environment as
a problem of fixed dimensions, in which as in the relatively
clear world of mathematics one locates the precise parameters of uncertainty and then specifies them in a formula
that, when followed correctly, yields full understanding —

this happy concept is less than satisfactory in dealing with the subtle behavioral impulses of a complex organism maintaining itself within an equally complex milieu. The mathematician's field of exact measurements gives way to the relative confusions of behavior beyond the range of cause-effect definition. Even the relations that one does feel can be spoken of are in some degree unspecifiable. As I pursue these investigations by the process of dialectic — the only tool for such an effort — even that process turns back on itself and deceives us. We are often caught in contemporary forms of that ancient philosophic tangle, the infinite regress. But we retain at least the following hold on reality as it affects our nervous systems and view of the future: the sure knowledge of our shrinking earthly supports as the race increases rapidly in number and of our own limited powers of adaptability in the face of swift and violent change. It is this knowledge that fixes our comprehensive frame of reference when we speak of environment and environmentalism. And this knowledge, axiomatically, forces us one important step further: to consider more critically our own behavior in this finite world we inhabit.

The behavior of man toward physical nature can be only one part of the problem of environmental behavior. We have also to consider the behavior of man toward other men and the behavior of man toward himself. Besides the factor of physical relations, there are also the social and psychological ones to deal with. These are all elements in a complicated, infinitely varied pattern of adjustments among the totality of elements making up man's universe. Facing the challenge of such complex and threatening stimuli, each individual looks for some sheet anchor by which to hold to a steady course in an otherwise limitless flux of experience. Environmental response and the environmental outlook, as defined here, offer a person one focus, one *Weltanschauung*, that can maximize his sense of self-direction while at the same time helping to preserve man's fundamental contract with nature.

To sum up, an environmental sense must involve a delicate sense of balance. That sense the individual must achieve for himself; it cannot be ready-made for him. Today's efficient information-gathering and monitoring services have provided a glut of data to complicate the individual's efforts at achieving that sense of balance. The more he reads and hears, the more complex his efforts must become. Aware man now knows the dangers his activities pose to both his earthly and his spatial supports. He knows that a return to a primitive hunting economy, or turning the clock backward in some other engineered way, will make matters worse, not better. He is committed to a claim that demands continued nurture from his surroundings while he pursues his search for self-fulfillment. The environmental sense will not be attained if the individual cannot learn to balance just such elements of contradiction. And lacking this environmental sense, this ability to maintain a precarious but necessary balancing act, man's behavior becomes anti-environmental.

Learning, if it bears the relevance to behavior that behavioral sciences claim, offers a principal avenue to controlled change, perhaps the one major option for conquering fear and the shocks of repeated change, for *dealienating* the species. But learning is linked inextricably with an organism's environment. The art of living implies a corresponding art of adaptation. To adapt, in the environmental sense, will mean to open all possible gates to the balanced learning of which I have spoken. A challenge, yes. But not an impossibility.

2
The Basis of
Environmental Education

We are witnessing in these later decades of the twentieth century the beginning of a trend that will reshape conditions of life in the twenty-first-century world in a remarkable way. This trend, for lack of any as-yet accepted nomenclature, may be termed a recognition, in the form of a growing mass movement toward ecological sanity, that very strict limits on all forms of human production and consumption, as well as on handling of waste, have become necessary if the human race is to continue developing as a viable species.

In all industrialized countries the literate populations have already become aware of the failure of man to achieve a balanced relationship with his environment. Unfortunately, those who have attained this state of awareness are but a small minority of the planet's total population. To the extent that ignorant masses in underdeveloped lands have set as a primary goal the duplication of Western living standards, any future solution of the basic problem on a global scale has been made all the more difficult.

31

There exists, in short, a crisis of adjustment between man and his natural environment wherever one looks in the world. History reveals what forces and how many have acted in concert to thrust the human organism into its present difficult situation. But it is education, a new form of education, that perhaps offers the one available means of finding a way out of the impasse.

Our current environmental crisis has its roots in man's earliest dabblings in technology. However, only with the advent of the Industrial Revolution have elements of technological growth and the technological point of view culminated in full-scale destruction of environmental supports needed for the maintenance of balance among the world's living communities. And only in the post-World War II period has man's appetite for rapine and extravagance been linked totally with the use of exploitative technology, to the end that race self-destruction itself now looms over humankind as never before.

Humanity's ability to survive, nevertheless, may be deliberately underestimated by the newly arrived seers of the ecology industry, who with a few random glances at certain statistical projections have made themselves and their readers wholly knowledgeable regarding the kind of fate man must surely meet some decades farther on into the future. In the patently negative approach taken by these journalists and publicists, it has proved necessary to emphasize a "no-way-out" syndrome. From the social-psychological point of view, it remains entirely within the realm of possibility that such a carefully nurtured spirit of despair may indeed in the end create all the proper conditions of a self-fulfilling prophecy: man will be unable to prevent the ultimate disaster, not because he has failed to master his environment but because he has failed to master himself.

This view, however, overlooks the possibilities inherent in educational measures that might be taken to alleviate the adverse pressures driving man to race suicide. Legitimate environmental education promises a means of stabilizing in the future both the sociopsychological and physical aspects of the current retrograde situation. The problem consists not so much in why or whether such instruction should be given (these questions cannot in conscience be answered negatively), but in *how* environmental sanity can be taught successfully. How, in particular, can the public schools, which alone among our social institutions reach a majority of future citizens at a crucial formative stage, be employed fairly yet effectively in this enterprise? Following in the American tradition, much grass-roots activity in this direction is already underway in formal classroom settings and informally among school youth and their teachers. Administrators too are taking an interest in the possibility of installing independent courses centered upon environmental learning in both pre-college and college curricula.

But there remains unsettled the larger issue that these movements reflect. Serious questions are raised for which no ready answers are available: Can the schools alone reeducate a seemingly profligate consumer society? What alternative models should be considered as we try to build a different future social order? No matter what social agencies finally carry out the teaching that will inculcate environmental behavior, how can the job be done so as to heal, rather than further widen, the social and economic divisions within society that have contributed so much to the environmental crisis we face?

Difficulty of Achieving Consensus

America maintains a society built on an important principle: that men bring the broadest possible variety of influences to bear on a social problem and efforts to solve it. For this reason America has also become the social crucible of human conflict. Yet, at the same time this country serves as an exemplar of the best that has been achieved until now in the area of conflict resolution, relative in most cases, absolute and final in a few.

Juxtaposed agreement and disagreement continue to be built into most "solutions" of social problems. The paradoxical struggle between local and more global interests in education is a case in point. This struggle has, in fact, a clear bearing on setting directions for environmental learning, since one must in the first instance assess where in the socioeconomic order, whether at the local, intermediate, or national level, the key impetus toward needed change in mass attitudes may exist.

Localism has traditionally been the source of much of this nation's educational strength, as well as of its educational weakness. Social and political trends, however, have acted over recent decades to shift effective control over important aspects of educational decision-making to higher-level political units. This is a counterpart of change in the economic picture: there America has emerged from a nation of entrepreneurs and small, independent operators to become the world headquarters of corporate power. The parallel extends even further into the realm of economic organization. Large-scale unionism has arisen to form a complement to big business among the labor force. In the mass society, rank-and-file independence of maneuver, the right to make final decisions on a local level, the ability to behave as if the theory of decentralization were one with its practice — these have gone the way of the Stanley Steamer in essentially every area of organized social life.

Despite occasional evidence to the contrary, education as a social institution has been moving in the same direction. Local boards and administrations look to those higher in prestige in the mass society (e.g., to "recognized experts," researchers, persons highly placed in an appropriate government bureau, etc.) for guidance before taking action on even minor questions. Decisions affecting education, therefore, as with business and politics, tend to become, in fact if not in name, the preserve of increasingly fewer individuals representing ever-larger bodies of "constituents."

Education thus resembles great corporations or labor unions

in respect to the decision-making process. With a free market in thought an established fact of life and with fewer voices heard in the effective consideration of final decisions — a contradiction consistent with the ground rules of life in a mass democratic society — fear of upsetting the status quo tends to become a chief determinant of local as well as of national behavior. Interlocking elements within the system as a whole are recognized as being both quintessential to survival and of exceeding fragility, so that tampering with any part of the whole risks possible inordinate damage to all other parts. The result may be predicted with an increasing expectation of accuracy in statement: no decision, or the indefinite delay of a decision, will be the outcome in more and more cases. This dilemma is nowhere more clearly marked than in the contradictory approaches now being made by both local and national decision-makers in the American educational system with regard to the problem of environmental education.

Material growth and the increased consumption of material goods have been accepted as cornerstones of progress for several centuries in ruling Western business and political circles. Only in the last few years has a small, conscience-bound segment of Western society become alarmed over what continued despoilment of the physical environment augurs for future generations of citizens. While to date the energy spent in consideration of environmental problems has largely been spent establishing and then reestablishing that an environmental crisis does indeed exist, new views of priorities and new foci of interest have begun to emerge. A second phase in the struggle has begun. Now the issue of values in human existence has surfaced as a thread in the environmental dialogue. Thus far the good that has been accomplished in this second phase has been minimal; conflict has merely been intensified. Yet who can say that this conflict is not essential to progress in securing future environmental gains?

Realization of the value component of the problem may already have been given as much publicity as can be tolerated

by the general public. Time Magazine recently expressed the
case in these terms to its widespread readership:

> The environment may well be the gut issue that can unify a polarized
> nation in the 1970's. It may also divide people who are appalled by
> the mess from those who have adapted to it. No one knows how
> many Americans have lost all feeling for nature and the quality of life.[1]

Americans, and to a lesser extent members of every other
affluent Western society, are thus divided among and within
themselves over environmental policy. Although no one can
doubt the depth of this divisiveness and its contribution to a
worsening of the environmental crisis, insufficient thought
has been given to the role of education in bringing some
degree of stability into the situation. In particular, certain
basic questions relating to education must be put forward:
Given its internal value and organizational conflicts that
reflect those of the larger society, how can the American
educational structure fulfill any truly significant role in
furthering a solution to the environmental impasse? Can
that role, considering conditions presently obtaining, be at
this stage defined in any essentially functional terms?

A Broad-Scale Approach to the Problem

Teaching environmental sanity has been now aptly termed
a problem of primarily social, rather than technological,
dimensions. "Attention has too long been diverted from the
more fundamental question: how to implement what we
already know and how to choose rationallly among technical
alternatives and their alternative costs. The process of choos-
ing does not involve science. It is political and social."[2]
Teaching for such choice, and teaching for the necessary
political and social awareness, assume in effect the possibility of shifting the outlook of a mass population from one of
anthropocentrism to one of adaptation. The swiftness with

which such a shift can come about has been grossly exagera-
ted. It will not come about in one or two generations, or perhaps in a dozen. To be sure, plans must be made and they
must be implemented; but this can take place only over a
considerable spread of time. The ideology of endless growth
and technological exploitation for narrow purposes will
indeed be overthrown. But when this is to occur can certainly not be well calculated on the basis of present data. And
once this ideology is done away with, it must be replaced
with a difficult new science: the science of social design.[3]

If the prodigious undertakings these developments suggest
are to be carried out successfully, education must perform a
key role in the process. But it should also not be lost sight of
that in a certain measure it is reeducation that is involved —
a mass reeducation. No alternative tool will be available for
bringing about a modification of the behavioral patterns and
underlying emotional conditions so typical of the contemporary consumer-despoiler mass society.

It should be stated without hesitation at this point that
attainment of survival goals may involve in the educative
phase the use of measures that have heretofore been considered (at least by many purists in democratic societies, where
the luxury of free expression allows for many strange pro-
motions of personal points of view) unethical and irrational.
Indeed, we perhaps are rightly, as inheritors of the Enlightenment tradition of rational man, accustomed to scoff at
"propaganda" or "indoctrination" as suitable only for the
use of Nazis or Maoists. However, the argument that we have
been led into the present state of affairs and may be able to
work ourselves out again *only* through the use of such
irrational goads to behavior may have just enough truth in it
to warrant more than passing consideration.

We tend too easily to forget how thoroughly advertising
and the culture of never-satisfied wants have done their job.
Consider the difficulty of preparing a turnabout in a society
urged and accustomed to consume and reproduce without
stint or limit. The average man's acceptance of nature's

limitations, if he is a North American, has become extremely difficult to elicit. He has been "locked into a system that compels him to increase his herd without limit — in a world that is limited. Ruin is the destination toward which all men rush, each pursuing his own best interest. . . "[4] The question of using forms of indoctrination or propaganda to effect an about-face is under the circumstances academic. To avert self-destruction, should not the race be prepared to sacrifice means to ends?

In an American school system presently wavering between the traditional canons of local control and the emerging reality (not as yet given full legal sanction) of rule by experts and/or nationally influential institutions, society may not find ready to hand the effective tool of change that another system of education, one based on other traditions and standards, might have represented. But of necessity the society is forced to act; it is taking the first groping steps toward inculcating a new mass orientation vis-à-vis the environment. Even given our current ignorance, we will in due course launch those programs through which the millions yet to be born will learn, before they learn anything else, that consensus regarding man's home, the earth, and its treatment must be reached before any human being is turned loose in search of individual pleasures, or to seek indeed what have heretofore been regarded as inalienable and undeniable personal rights.

There will be hard choices ahead. One cannot minimize the difficulty of the organizational work that lies in the offing. One can scarcely overstate it. What must be devised amounts to no less than the development of a theoretical framework that will support a fully operative educational mechanism by which the basic attitudes of that entire portion of the human family yet to arrive on this planet will be changed, turned around nearly full circle. The prospect is indeed staggering. Educational policy setters, at all levels but especially the national, will perform delicate and essential roles in this undertaking. In the earlier stages of this task experimentation, confusion, and mistrust are likely to prevail. Yet, without leadership that can carry on through such an intitial period of difficulty, there will be grave doubt over humanity's future status on this planet. In the world of educators, both professional and nonprofessional, such leadership exists.

The policymaker in education holds a master key to any relatively successful orientation of the mass society to many sweeping changes soon to appear. This is true for the reason that in one form or another only education can bridge the gap "between an ordered society and those who reject not only the solutions but, more importantly, the problem-solving mechanisms of the ordered society."[5]

The call is made to those who have strength, those who are ready. Can they rise to the challenge?

3

Environmental Learning: A Cooperative Approach via the Socioeconomic Power Center

The late twentieth century may be characterized as a period of human transition, a few decades in which to prepare society for the radically new era of the twenty-first century. Some time after the year 2,000 man will achieve a more constant and fully defined relationship with his sociophysical milieu. By then the establishment of human behavioral autonomy within the concretely understood limits imposed by nature will signify a stage in man's evolution comparable to that of his emergence from the ape. But in those few decades of changeover, social difficulties will appear to increase rather than diminish.

At a time when unwanted humans are arriving in increasing numbers and man lives under conditions of growing stress and turmoil as he drives toward the unavoidable target point of environmental balance, education as a key element in the struggle for *positive* integration becomes needed as never before. Experiences multiply in number; they converge upon the individual with great psychological force and from innumerable directions. Formal and informal sources of learning are totally intertwined, yet all must be taken into account. Policies must be set and decisions made. Indefensible *laissez-faire* attitudes, continued acts of omission, making decisions that are wrong because they "solve" the wrong problem,[1] the *de facto* results of our refusal to recognize the extent to which our habit of following Parkinson's Law has made us too conscious of a need to keep busy and not enough aware of a need to develop human potentials — all these will be but some of the bedrock policy issues in education with which all society (not merely the community of formal educators) must grapple as industrialized man approaches the next stage of his evolution as a species.

Creating learning situations that are adequate for the needs of individuals in this period of swift change involves making decisions that take into account all the potentially viable social units: the individual himself, his family and circle of acquaintances, the formal educational system, and the corporate state as it carries on various educative functions. In the following discussion those emerging trends and conditions which seem likely to effect significant change, educationally speaking, within and through each of these units will be considered.

The Individual: Trends and Imperatives

Self-indulgence seems likely to become in the later twentieth century an increasingly expensive and dangerous practice, in both its individual and societal manifestations, if by self-indulgence is meant the continuing cultivation of tastes for pleasures that require the exploitation of persons, objects, or resources physically separate from the person(s) seeking the experience of such pleasure. The conspicuous consumer, accountable to no one for his actions, already may be proceeding the way of the dodo bird — appearances and easily visible cultural atavisms to the contrary. But cooperative endeavor in the pursuit of those experiences which permit the person to increase his psychological grip on social reality will find increasing favor, in the sense particularly that stubborn adherence to the more arbitrary inequalities of the old social order will give way to a new vigor in the group search for right social action. Essentially, the pleasure principle will not have been negated; it will have been transferred from a simpler to a more complex operating level, from a physical, animal, or noncognitive base to an integrative, reasoned, adaptive, more psychically flexible base.

The individual's existential predicament will not happily disappear; in fact, the specter of overcrowding and overcompetition for scarce resources and what will have become the many necessaries of existence in an affluent industrial society seems likely to place the individual even more in the position of not being able to escape himself. In the evolutionary process through which succeeding gererations must pass, in a speeded-up version of historical development as previously known, the successful adapter will be characterized by his effective effort to achieve vital life satisfactions from individual and cooperative ventures less and less related to the typical animal appetites alone.

The emotional duel between the dramatic figures of Blanche and Stanley in *A Streetcar Named Desire* will become increasingly inappropriate as a model of the essential struggle within the human psyche and in interpersonal relations. Neither fey day-dreaming nor bullish masculinity can easily survive in a real world of imperatives toward positive adaptation, although for some time to come, in the absence of alternative concepts of human purpose that can be successfully communicated to the industrial masses, people will hang on grimly to the false statement that an emotion sublimated is a right denied. Indeed, much color will have been removed from public life when alcoholic actresses, political careerists, or condemned felons who can reach the mass audience via a cooperative, publicity-exploiting medium can no longer interest audiences in their display of private feelings. But this loss will, or can be, made up in the color that attaches to the enriching efforts and activities of self-development, although the social point of reference must in this case give way to a more idiosyncratic context of experience, perhaps in the personalist-individualist tradition of such liberal educators as Shaftesbury and Humboldt.

For the individual who is pliant without conceding loss of personality, the challenge of self-development will also create a counterweight to the threat of existential oblivion. In this phase of man's psychological evolution, unreasonable pressures to conform to social norms will be overcome by the individual who, in the existential context, adds to his conscious behavior an adaptive focus. Psychologically speaking, this is a person who can steadily move forward in the development of complementary yet contrasted skills of living: the ability to turn always further into himself for psychic growth and the ability to identify with an ever-broadening segment of the world intellectual community. This person possesses as well a capacity for maximizing the one while constrained for periods of time to do without the other — a necessary capability in an age of dislocations and social confusions.

Much fear is expressed that excessive homogeneity in human life styles will become widespread in the post-industrial future. Communist China is seen as a model of what all societies will inevitably be like. This is a logical enough assumption, perhaps, but not necessarily a logical outcome. Society's inner balance in the near future of the next several decades depends on its ability to accommodate to two primary sources of strain: drastic physical-resource limitation, and frustration among the many not naturally endowed with those gifts needed to make the most of an inevitable new direction in living. What will indeed be lacking are the flamboyance and outward contrasts of the old society, in which excess of wealth or poverty, or of display directed exclusively to the securing of some social effect, constituted the outwardly and popularly significant characteristics of life-style. The new life-style, centered in the main around an individual process of intellection and personal growth, will present few such impressive outward manifestations, and this may be just as well. Envy of the endurance and moral standing of this prototype of future man, if it became sufficiently widespread, might destroy those transitional social forms which will permit if not encourage its continued existence.

The individual who is both free and responsible in the greatest degree has, as one thread of Maslow's work implies,[2] no remaining need of supports within a group or a culture by which to prop up his ego and maintain his psychological fitness. Praise and blame, like and dislike, assume the nature of social exercises that merely indicate the extent to which interpersonal or intergroup communication breaks down against the ego-free mentality of the psychologically mature individual. The latter is then remarkably well suited to hold himself aloof from the ordinary "trials and tribulations" of life and concentrate upon fulfillment tasks as he perceives them. He is, in fact, the model of environmentally adapted man.

The view of freedom-cum-responsibility as a primarily psychological condition of attainment cannot help but be reinforced as modern societies themselves adapt to and begin to engineer new employment structures better suited to human sociopsychic needs in a post-technological era. Throughout the history of industrialism to date, the dominating motive in the use of men to maintain any system of production has been the concept of "finding a man who fits the job." In post-industrial society, with the established success of social engineering and the "third-phase" psychological evolution among individuals as accepted facts of group life, jobs will be, at long last, more clearly designed "to fit the individual man, or woman." Nevertheless, this will prove no easy millennial stage for man to reach. There will be the harsh transitional period to live through, for one thing. This transition, in fact, should prove the ultimate testing-time, for in it the individual will find himself less and less able to exist through the aid of old artificial props to the ego. Sociopsychological detection of all the once-hidden corners of existence goes on apace, and it is in the nature of the technological society to destroy by exploitation whatever maintains itself on a basis of weakness rather than strength. Integration in terms of the current evolutionary process cannot permit exceptions to the new rules of natural selection.

In the world of transitional tomorrow, the person incapable of steady intellectual growth will not simply inhabit the dustbins of society. This truism applies only to today. Our great contemporary effort to assist the numerous physically damaged members of the species through special education, prosthetic devices, mental hospitals, and the like, is essentially a holding action. It allows an emotionally immature society to expend its excess of self-justification on the most readily available objects of pity. It is an action geared to make life as tolerable as possible for those rendered by uncontrolled breeding or by social error incapable of living what is otherwise deemed a "full" existence. Such conditions cannot continue indefinitely in a world subject to steadily more effective rationalization of every human resource. In due time society is likely to accept that health technology must bring to a halt the production of grossly unfit types. Tomorrow's unfit will not exist; they will remain unborn.

A complex environment demands, as the Darwinian formula implies, adaptation of a species according to inviolable laws of development and change.[3] Freedom for individuals, in such a complicated milieu of crowding and uncertainty, cannot very well resemble the "freedom" known in earlier, easier times. The individual who will thrive under these new circumstances will be the person who finds freedom within himself. But in a society in which "other-directedness" has been woven so successfully into the entire fabric of life, this form of freedom has been limited to but a tiny percentage of the population. This life context, this necessary, adaptive individualism, to a greater number of humans will constitute the great goal of transitional social evolution. Man in the mass society becomes what he learns. Can the ordinary human being whose life is formed by his learning be assisted in achieving more of this essential self-direction? The question bids us inquire into the forces that direct this learning now, have directed it in the past, and will direct it in the future.

The Family and Circle of Acquaintances

In a look farther into the future than a few years, it may be suggested that radical changes in the individual's choice of a primary reference group seem likely to affect seriously his patterns of learning. It is important to recognize the difficulties posed for individuals of whatever intellectual capacity in learning adaptive and environmentally sound behaviors as once fixed but now steadily deteriorating social reference points give way to less-certain and more conflict-ridden foci. The lack of available or effective substitute reference points to take the place of family, neighborhood structure, and work or other local affinity groups formerly providing sources for individual allegiance and identification implies an intermediate period of particular maladjustment and friction. In essence, rootlessness will dominate the human picture in advanced societies for some time to come and can only leave in its wake a temporarily unintegrated populace, seeking for some new lodestar of connectedness to the universe.[4]

At the heart of this destruction of the individual's one-time stable frame of social reference lies the communications revolution. This revolution has, to an extent not fully appreciated, succeeded in breaking down practically all the old configurations of interpersonal and intersocial influence on individual behavior. The significance of direct person-to-person contacts in social-psychological terms has been drastically reduced. The "significant other" will no longer, in a typical case, be a person with whom one shares a bed or the morning and evening meals. It will more likely be a "superstar" promoted to an undeniable place of prominence in the mass psyche, or a superior dimly viewed during working hours through the subtle, constricting social screen erected by corporate chains of command and informal "pecking orders."

The opportunity to manipulate the new communications technology to direct individual interests and allegiances becomes daily more impossible to resist. This situation has created inordinate pressures upon the person receiving stimuli. In comparison with his grandparents, any youth today, encouraged by the multifaceted media, has a vastly wider range of options to pursue in seeking information and experience. The dissatisfactions of family living drive him inevitably away from those situationally closest to him. This is not merely a matter of self-encouragement in a Walter Mitty type of daydream by which one transports himself mentally beyond the immediate horizon. In any developed country the physical mobility of an increasing proportion of the population means necessarily that, in a given single lifetime, constant replacement of one acquaintance, life-companion, or interest group by others must become an accepted and ubiquitous practice. The problem for the individual arises from the fact that he is able to choose from a theoretically unlimited number of potential inter-personal contacts or reference groups, yet this range of choice is in fact ever more strictly limited by the operational tactics of those forces controlling the communications revolution in its main social thrusts. Communications systems have, in short, acted as much to prohibit formation of significant new forms of social contact as they have to destroy old ones.

It would seem futile to argue against the belief that for some while into the future the communications revolution will remain a tool in the hands of socioeconomically established elites. One may cite the current rage for corporate mergers, involving among others the communications industry, as primarily a means of facilitating larger profits. But while this phenomenon does provide a *prima facie* explanation of the current drive for diversification among all corporations, it may also indicate implicit recognition by the communications industry of the steadily increasing difficulty of operation under the economy-of-scale principle while serving a constantly more individualized (and consequently less rationally exploitable) market. In effect, the current mass audience may be disintegrating even as a dozen grandiose conglomerates of the industry appear to be making their most successful bid in recorded memory for the exploitation of a few vehicles for massive profit.

Thus, monopoly may have achieved only a temporary victory. With the breakdown of local and family influences, a vacuum was left to be filled and into it flowed the ubiquitous media like water through a broken weir. Still, humanity's doubts remain; the public is aware that bestsellers or "superstars" are created by a PR system rather than through any natural social process. The controls exerted by a centrally operated communications system are effective because they use a technology that precludes the intrusion of countervailing forces — they are *not* effective because people truly believe in their message.

In any case, local and family groups or contacts are substantively bypassed by the unmediated, one-way communications between the controlled sources of stimuli and the individual on the receiving end. Even peer-group influence as a foremost determinant of individual behavior must be viewed in a proper perspective. A phenomenon such as

teenage rock-and-roll music would not exist if there were no
central organs of controlled communication to insure its
maximum stimulation of every teenager capable of interacting with his peers within this "musical" context. The peer
group of whatever age does not necessarily originate or
control its own behavior; it more often simply serves as a
lateral reinforcer of those actions. There is a great difference
between the actual invention of stimuli by which sociopsychic behavior is initiated and the mechanical diffusion of
those stimuli to ever-more widespread elements within society.

The breakdown of local and family groups as *effective*
sharing units in an independent decision-making process
leaves a gap in the transmission of culture that has as yet not
been adaquately filled. To bridge this gap is not necessarily
the task of a movement toward "environmentalization" of
learning and behavior. In a technical sense the gap may no
longer be, in fact, capable of being filled. Communications
technology has brought the dominant, socially rationalized
culture of capitals of politics and fashion to the remotest
hamlets. Any truly environmental approach to human social
problems cannot be based on the assumption that this trend
must be reversed; it cannot find its *raison d' être* in any
scheme to turn back the clock. The "ordeal of change"
(to borrow Eric Hoffer's well-chosen term) is a concept that
rules out the mere literal repetition of past experience; the
true environmental thinker sees past experience as at best
a suspect guide, but the only available one to a perilous
future.

The suggestion that family, friendship-group, and other
social elements largely local and situational in makeup and
influence can or should ever again function in the old way
seems unreasonable. The sources of control over mass behavior have shifted away from this level. To attain any grasp
whatever of the future course of group living one must
examine the workings of the corporate state itself. In this
examination the student is advised to keep in mind the
twin and antagonistic influences bearing on the corporate

decision-making process. These are, on the one hand, the necessary maintenance of a leadership function in society (to obviate, among other things, assumption of power by socially retrograde elements — the extremists, incompetents, and so forth) and, on the other, society's undeniable right to determine as much as it can the course of its own evolution.

Society and Education: The Clouded Present

In the model of contemporary democratic Scandinavia, we observe the relative homogenization of external social life and (not without certain pains of adaptation) an implicit, continuing effort of the organized society to force the individual inward upon himself as a necessary group function in the process of social evolution. This situation parallels in some degree what Lecomte du Noüy saw as the developmental cycle working itself out in a three-stage universal evolutionary progression, with humanity now groping its way into the third, or psychological, stage. (The theory holds "that the evolutionary force of the cosmos, having spent itself in the inorganic [cosmological] and organic [Darwinian biological] sectors of the cosmos, will now come to a halt in those areas and shift to the psychological. The earth has finished evolving and man, as an animal, has arrived at the limit of his physiological development. But psychologically man is just beginning to evolve".[5]) In any event, one can see how in the prototype societies of modern Scandinavia moderate socialism gradually erodes the traditions of solipsist behavior and, however successfully, nudges the individual into new, apparently more adaptive modes of behavioral adjustment.

In contrast to this picture of effective social pressures on the individual in such relatively homogeneous cultures stands the more extreme model of uninhibited American capitalist society. In its most primitive forms, this system seems to have the effect at times of socially degenerating certain elements within society to such an extent that nearly all behavior of those individuals affected involves conscious effort at heterogeneity. Although suicide may in Sweden represent a conscious rejection of social pressure aimed at forcing the individual inward upon his own resources, in America suicide may well signify something rather different: an ultimate attempt to secure social *approbation,* possible in a culture that has overstressed the importance of individualism shown in the social gesture of nonconformity, even at the price of personal survival. In both cases, of course, rejective behavior is an expression of nonintegration of the individual with society and it indicates a transitional phase of social development. In the environmental sense, it is more important to see that a common thread runs through the whole list of instances in which citizens of such diversely governed states as the U.S.A., Sweden, the U.S.S.R., France, Japan, and so on regularly take their own lives: this is the apparent *inevitability* of suicide (and of a good many dozen other familiar phenomena of retrograde individual behavior) within the social structure of the corporate enterprise as presently practiced and understood.[6]

This would never be so if it were not that the evolution to "phase three" of the universal evolutionary process constitutes an extraordinary psychic and organizational barrier to human progress. In one of its principal manifestations the problem, which in its most general aspect involves getting humanity safely *across* this barrier, consists in getting people out to the boundary limits where change can actually take place, and then fighting against their natural tendency toward retrogression, keeping them there until change has in fact occurred. It appears that any effort to explain resistance to or acceptance of change solely in terms of economics or of a specific political system that oversees an economy is an excessively narrow effort, one doomed to failure. One can in the first instance only examine the multiplicity of influences that bear upon the functioning of the outward regulator of life in modern society, that is, the corporate entity, and in the second, see them radiate back out from that entity in a reciprocal counterinfluence upon the workings of society itself.[7] In this matter one should not lose sight of the possible effects of the corporate form of social organization upon man as a learner as well as an inhabitant of the natural environment.

In one of its aspects, this problem forces a return to the issue of how best to enforce social progressivism in any given society. The more simplistic subissues (e.g., redistribution of wealth) cannot be permitted to confuse the larger issue. In this respect education tends, under optimum conditions, literally to come into its own. One might begin by examining a particular socioeconomic order, for example, the U.S.A. It may be said that extremes of wealth and poverty, as exemplified in the "best" of American traditions, are apparently inevitable as a means of maintaining for at least the historical present an investment-intensive economy. Unemployment and inflation, along with the host of allied socioeconomic ills, must then be debated at length. But after this much of the course has been run, one begins to lean toward a hard but not illogical generalization: this post-industrial form of an undiluted corporate economy is itself subject to change, is itself evolving into constantly newer forms, and social adjustment to this evolution becomes a learning, rather than merely a political, or economic problem.

There is a reciprocal burden that the elite must share with other members of society in this learning process. In its efforts to "explain" unwarranted concentrations of power and wealth or the persistence of poverty, the corporate state, East or West, bears an additional responsibility: to give evidence that it supports popular education by which the progressive democratization and sharing of corporate wealth and authority can eventually be realized. This is a learning experience for all involved. Of course, part of what is learned will involve recognition by all concerned of the preferability of evolutionary change over debilitating spasms of violence as a means of moving society forward. But an equally important outcome of this social learning must be that it leads to a concerted and continuous pressure upon leadership, the pressure of a multitude of minds bent on the ideal of evolutionary change in the direction of environmental social justice. This amounts to nothing less than developing the inherent potentiality of the corporate entities as agencies of mass learning. This does not imply a repetition of past experience in making the masses as malleable as possible in the interests of a monolithic elite. Realism appears to fall on the side of those who see mass learning as becoming essentially a growingly complex but also ever more necessary element in the social development of all modern societies. The dictum that the more intimidating a state's control mechanisms, the simpler the manipulation of mass learning, clearly does not hold any longer. Conditions of life in, for example, the U.S.S.R. seem to indicate that, even under a forceful and technically skilled despotism, management of learning intended to result in widespread compliant behavior fails in its psychological aspect – and this even when the coercive power of the corporate state has reached theoretically unlimited physical proportions. Thus, both in Russia and the West, the subtle demands of the individual for recognition *as himself* override in their social-psychological effect any imposition of monolithic powers of coercion. This opposition seems, in fact, to become the stronger for being subjected to the more odious forms of socioeconomic rationalization. In both cases the restriction of decision-making power to constantly smaller units and fewer individuals (e.g., the Politburo, the executive of any Western corporation) acts as a patently social-psychological retrogression, a perhaps necessary but unpopular restraint in the evolution toward a more environmentally adaptive mode of social life.

The destruction of unwarranted monolithic control is, nevertheless, despite outward appearances, underway wherever sufficient social pressure can be brought to bear on decision-makers to temper their actions with a sense of environmental imperatives. The spreading realization of how great complexity is involved in making fair judgments of

even seemingly minor interpersonal or intergroup issues
constitutes an implicit acceptance of the principle of environmentally based responsibility, that is, that responsibility
which is in the highest degree both social and individual and
a balance of the two.

> Mankind's salvation lies exclusively in everyone making everything
> his business, in the people of the East being anything but indiffer-
> ent to what is thought in the West, and in the people of the West
> being anything but indifferent to what happens in the East.[8]

The corporate entities of any advanced society (whatever
formal rubric they fall under, government, business, labor,
philanthropic foundation, etc.) can never be fully responsive
to all the needs of all components of that society, including
the single individual, without possessing some means by
which to measure comprehensively the extent to which
their corporate advantage in any given instance clashes with
legitimate social-individual interests. Here again the power of
communications technology and the directions that such
power can take require consideration. The glut of information about which even the technicians of cybernated society
today complain will, for good or evil and almost without
public notice, turn from a flood into a tidal wave when full
social realization of the need of the race for balance among
its members and in relation to its planetary support systems
is reached. Demand for information will gradually rise to the
point at which the whole literate public should be able to
control all substantive social decision-making, through group
control over an information system so comprehensive that,
at least for those citizens whose educational level is sufficient, a kind of consensus politics unknown in past history
will become the norm. But this highly desirable state of
affairs is still far distant on the social horizon.

Corporate control of both the generation of information
and its dissemination will, in the meantime, create strains of
adjustment within a society only sluggishly evolving at this
point toward new standards of individual and group behavior.

As we move on into the changeover era, this means increasing popular pressure to use all sources of information service for the ultimate welfare of society as a whole. It also probably means a continuance and possible stepping-up of counterpressure, at least for the short term, as various elements within the clique of old-time would-be monopolists seek and find unusual means for maintaining their time-honored, parochial dominance over portions of the information flow, such as "slanting" of the news by various media writers or commentators.

As the 1970s witness a gathering momentum for change society-wide, public dissatisfaction is focussed on public education. While innovations in educational technology occupy the interest of most schoolmen themselves, critics with less occupation-centered concerns are zeroing in on broader issues in policymaking. Works such as the Rand Report "How Effective Is Schooling?" (1972) and studies by Greer and Jencks[9] tend to show a cumulative disillusion over the failure of schools in America to perform as agents of social reform, a disillusion reflecting, apparently with considerable accuracy, the feelings of the inarticulate masses whose children are educated in public schools. Society is seemingly rethinking the whole question of what schools can do and what they should be expected to do. Age-old assumptions are being challenged and the challenge is backed up with evidence; change that will be more than nominal is inevitable, but the question is one of when and under what circumstances.

One of the old assumptions on which society has operated is that which maintains a belief in school-plus-family as providing sufficient experience to the neophyte to allow him to make his way in society. Consider this belief in relation to the children of lower-class families in the U.S. Research studies on the academic aptitudes of these children are revealing: there are large numbers of low-status children with superior intellectual potential growing up in conditions of poverty, both economic and intellectual; possibly as many as one-forth of all slum children in northern cities have an I.Q. of 109 or higher.[10] One black educator estimates that on the basis of population data for 1966 (government figures, from the 87th Annual Statistical Abstract of the U.S.) some "4,000,500 slum children possess *above average* intelligence as compared to 3,000,500 upper-class white children."[11]

These data seem to suggest strongly that, in terms of life opportunities actually available to the slum children and in full recognition of the increasing difficulty early exclusion from learning experiences will pose for such children in their career progress, schooling is actually doing what extremist critics like Silberman and Holt claim — insuring that the child from deprived surroundings will carry additional burdens through his life instead of fewer. (This is not the same as to say, it should be carefully noted, that schools cannot be highly valuable institutions under circumstances that redefine their relationships to the larger society, and vice-versa.) From the environmental standpoint, in which the race's long-term welfare within a physical system must be given more serious consideration, the contemporary schooling process is not so much socially negative as socially inefficient, since in the present stage of social evolution the artificial protection afforded a less capable element of society (e.g., low-ability upper-class youth) in the struggle to be rid of vestigial ignorance is offered precisely at the expense of the more capable element (e.g., high-ability slum children). Society thus, in its automatic resistance to change, where such resistance is possible, slows its own evolution toward "third-stage" psychosocial adaptation. By holding closed the opportunity structure, it confuses its priorities, preferring to work for preservation of a particular social class and standing fast for the time being against healing but psychologically disturbing change.

Under these circumstances the formal education system simply serves to reinforce social-class and economic-status divisions, rather than effecting socioeconomic mobility, needed today to a far greater degree than in the older, more slowly developing societies of the historical past. Still, the limits of the contemporary system of formal education to aid in bringing about change may not, even under present adverse conditions, prove so compelling as the new generation of educational critics feels must be the case. The pessimism of these critics, however well founded in fact, does serve a certain useful purpose at this point: it forces greater attention upon the informal agencies of education, especially the communications infrastructure as it spreads through the corporate system. It is well to keep in mind the extent to which this structure already, thanks to the rapid strides in recent decades of communications technology, successfully controls the context of a good deal of the learning and behavior, individual and social, local and society-wide, that take place today in any advanced society.

A Future Direction in the Management of Change in Learning

Of one thing we can be reasonably sure in all this matter: the critical power by which to channel countervailing elements for change in communications policy does not rest with the lowly public servants who work in or administer public schools. This power, and the responsibility that such power entails, rest with those who set policy for corporate enterprise, governmental or private. However, since government (except in the ultra-Marxian communist states) serves by definition as a kind of referee or neutral agent of arbitration between contending private parties who actually engage in the exploitative or service works in question, and since government does not initiate social reform or new directions in social growth without first ascertaining that enough elements of the private sector appear to desire such change, private corporate entities are by and large the more logical agencies for initiating majors shifts in such social undertakings as education. If the focus of change in mass learning and behavior is to be the organization of a *planned* shift that carries the whole society along in its informal thrust (e.g., toward a more environmental mass behavior), then the organized business community alone has the resources and, once its leadership is convinced of the need, a suitable infrastructure capable of bringing about realization of such an aim.

At present it is fashionable for people to adopt a kind of cross-grained view of that subsector of the business world that has taken mass communications for its exclusive corporate interest. One hears "the media" referred to as a sort of composite of all possible propaganda organs, a primarily malevolent institution able to form the mass psyche in any shape it chooses but especially that which keeps interest (and the cash flow) high through a conditioning process that suggests the tycoons of TV and publishing view the public as they would Pavlov's dogs. True, media executives maintain an attitude of strict commercialism in their long-range decision-making. But this is hardly a simon-pure, never-say-die, old-style commercial stance. The "public interest," however loosely defined, has its place in the media scheme of things. American television audiences, for example, would be expected to complain briskly if documentaries on social problems or special coverage of political events were removed from their screens. It is not the media dictatorship that stands in the way of a more comprehensive service of the public interest; it is the limitations of the media, instead, that create the problem.

Because the media devote so much viewing time, newsprint, and effort to entertainment or, equally significant, to perversity, and since these productions supposedly cater to the baser urges of a mass of citizens,[12] it is axiomatic that media decision-makers stand condemned in the eyes of the self-righteous. How could it be otherwise, for do not media policies serve to reinforce the kind of learning that debases the individual and his motives and pictures society as incapable of moral progress? Yet, on a larger view this single-minded understanding of the media possesses a greater share of falsehood than of truth. The falsehood lies in one's acceptance of the assumption that a kind of natural "devil's compact" has been arrived at between those who produce and those who consume. What this assumption overlooks is not so much the lack of alternatives within the media sector itself as the lack of alternative *outside* experiences for the consuming masses, experiences that could succeed with equal effect in creating vicarious interest and enjoyment and also be satisfying in a deeper, psychic sense — the individual sense.

The only viable source for generation of these outside experiences is the business sector itself. This having been said, the difficulties of securing cooperation both across corporate lines and within individual companies must be recognized. One point of argument relates to the need for corporate growth and development beyond the mere survival-profitability dimension. Here the point that needs to be made over and over, until the corporate mentality divests itself of the old, fixed mode of thinking, is that excess investment profit should be made available for *social* instead of for private development.

As corporations become fewer and markets are enlarged, a phenomenon that might be termed the "marginally fluctuating buying public" drastically alters the terms of competition in any business. When there are only two or three manufacturers of a product, each tends to come into control of a relatively stable segment of the market for that product. The struggle becomes then not one of survival but rather one of petty jockeying to see which one of the giants can edge out the others for the favor of the two or three percent of the buying public without advance commitment. For example, by strength of long tradition General Motors and its three major competitors control year by year a proportion of total American auto sales that can be estimated (assuming the availability of sufficient data for any given year and the computer resources to process such data) in advance with an accuracy approaching the absolute. G.M., in other words, has reason to project its sales and profits well into the future and so has every other major corporation — provided that new technologies do not inordinately disrupt usual marketing trends — with the result that decisions of large-scale social significance must be made with regard to how accumulating excess wealth may be used.

The recent growth of conglomerates shows the extent to which industry has already gone in diversifying its production and marketing as a kind of insurance policy to cover unlooked-for fluctuations in any single spectrum of commercial market activity. It will prove impossible for such diversification and mergers to go on indefinitely. Sooner or later this phase of the process of economic rationalization will come to an end, as soon as the principle has proven its ultimate usefulness. Long before then, it may be hoped, the corporate entity, recognizing fully its social and public functions, will have taken those steps which will set it even more firmly on the road to integration within the total complex of individual-state relationships. "If the mature corporation is . . . to be a part of the penumbra of the state, it will be more strongly in the service of social goals. It cannot plead its inherently private character or its subordination to the market as cover for the pursuit of different goals of particular interest to itself."[13]

The well-publicized work of E. F. Denison[14] has brought to public knowledge the important point that a nation's investment in formal schooling is an integral and determining indicator of that nation's rate of economic development. In general, this thesis holds that educational background "is a crucial determinant of the quality of labor . . . [it helps] to explain the differences between Europe and the United States . . . in levels of national income per person employed."[15] The greater the amount of investment in education (taken as a percentage of GNP), broadly speaking, the swifter the rate of internal economic development.

The diversity of educational backgrounds among Americans must be an advantage in that it provides broad opportunity to match the education of workers with educational requirements for specific types of work. The uniformity in education level of the great bulk of European workers may imply that individuals in the occupations least in need of educational background have more education than contributes much to job performance. It almost surely implies that in the most demanding occupations the European countries must often make do with workers having much less education than would be advantageous, or else they must be content with fewer workers in these occupations.[16]

This apparent advantage enjoyed by the United States over the countries of Western Europe in making greater variety in formal schooling (as well as greater availability) pay off economically must be seen, however, in the perspective of overall development. Another study, in which the role of education in national economic growth is probed in the developed-underdeveloped dimension, indicates that while returns to society from investment in education are greater than those from investment in physical capital for under-developed countries, the returns are the same for advanced countries.[17] Further, except for specialist fields perpetually lacking in adequate manpower, returns from education tend to diminish as one moves higher through the sequence of formal schooling and from less-developed through more-developed societies.[18] Higher education, for example, requires heavy investment, yet has a weak position in terms of economic payoff in the most advanced societies. Apparently a point can be reached at which any further investment in *formal* schooling will have minimal returns, from the purely economic standpoint. It is at this stage that new thinking at the level of corporate leadership can get societies as advanced as that of industrial North America to the entrance of the *new* society. The key concepts toward which an irresistible momentum will move those leaders will be: de-formalizing education; individualizing education; carrying education beyond the merely monetary-accountability aspect.

In fact, many corporate executives in the course of a

generation of management seminars have already been inch-
ing steadily nearer this enlarged view of the kind of education
appropriate to the real needs of thinking men in a late
industrial age, that is, a view that a man is more important
than what he produces and that, therefore, an education to
be of full value must enlarge the man's whole life outlook
rather than merely increase his competence in a single,
narrowly prescribed area. The existentialist philosopher's
unconcealed suspicion of man as a specialist will come to
have a greater acceptance on this view, but at the same time
the impractical outcomes of too literal an acceptance will be
tempered by both the common sense and the power to co-
erce that leadership in a cybernated society can never divest
itself of.

As the twentieth century wanes, as the complaints of
millions of workers fighting the constraints of unfulfilling
labor mount, as warnings such as those of Argyris and Fromm
against the dehumanization of industrial work undifferenti-
ated according to varying human psychic needs increasingly
come to pass[19] — sooner or later the necessity of establishing
a social power base for education *within* the industrial
system itself will be accepted. At this point the leading corporate entities, rich yet faced with unhappy public and labor
relations, may be expected to diversify into other than solely
profit-making enterprises. They will begin to create for their
workers and workers' families the kind of corporate counter-
force to the evils of unrewarded labor that only the scale
of accumulated industrial wealth will permit.

The corporate effort at this juncture will inevitably show
itself in start-stop fantasies and failures, but the very evident
need for action will force continuation of experimentation.
In due course, the effort will begin to flow into those forms
of activity which are best suited to meeting unfilled human
needs, especially once these can be defined in more than
rough terms (i.e., in human and individual rather than mere
arithmetic or accountancy values). The very existence on
paper of a scheme of this kind will, of course, provoke

strenuous objection. The separatist mentality will immediately complain that corporate provision of educational experience on other than job-related grounds interferes with the just balance of social functions as between the formal school system and the corporation. This claim may be rejected on two counts: first, the demand for extended, lifelong experience in education is greater than any formal school network could fulfill; second, the originality and creative radicalism of corporate ventures in education of adults and children will infuse the schools themselves with new ideas and cannot help but contribute significantly to social and individual growth, thus adding a new dimension of balance to social living in an age of excess leisure and the behavioral challenges that accompany it.

There is yet one more reason why the corporation should become the vanguard of educational development. It lies in the condition governing assembly-line work itself, and as such is directly related to the improvement of industrial life in the context of environmental imperatives. One cannot expect men forever to function as robots for eight hours a day, five days a week, without some compensation other than monetary. Significant learning, if made a part of the industrial process, can both ease the worker's way through life and restrain the buildup of his destructive reactions to the ennui under which he must labor. The extent of drug use on American assembly lines in the mid-1970s is a symptom, not a cause, and it serves as a warning to all concerned in the industrial enterprise — whether of the Marxist persuasion and advocating state control of means of production or of the school of thought that advocates continuance of the freely capitalist system — that different means of reinvesting profits, specifically in educationally valid, new forms of service to the workers' welfare cannot be developed by continuing, ostrichlike, to evade the core issue of worker alienation.

The movement toward bringing education into the industrial process is, then, and for reasons that should at this point be quite obvious, vital to the environmentalization of society. But like all change, and especially like the radical change this development represents, such a movement will not begin easily. The first line of resistance, that which the corporate boardroom constitutes, has already to some extent been penetrated. From this point forward progress should be steady but slow. Beginning experimentally and very tentatively, the movement should gradually gather momentum, to emerge after a time as an established force and chief bulwark against the parallel and also developing "technical barbarism" of that future era.[20] It will by then have become industry's principal form of insurance against the psychic breakdown of a society that has still to pass the barrier to effective futurism.

All this being the case, society has a vested interest in encouraging such a development, and industry has an interest in the same degree, for this is a prime means of better integrating industry with the body social that nourishes it. One of the important side benefits will be the emergence of a sociopsychic climate far better suited to the establishment of a working match between man and his physical environment. It will have proved no accident that this changed climate involves new and more adaptive behavior on the part of the industrial masses. But such behavior must in the first instance and in some way have been learned.

Some Possibilities Within This Framework

Possessing not only the fiscal but also the human resources to bring about this change of direction in social learning and behavior, the corporation even now stands ready as the catalytic agent for shaping a future more compatible with man's essential interests. Slowly the restraints to corporate entry onto the educational scene will fall, especially as leaders of industry realize the need to exert corporate initiative in developing individualized, informal mass education. At first view and to those altogether used to "things as they are," the idea of each corporation's, no matter what its principal business activity, promoting educational ventures on a fairly large scale seems absurd, a waste of shareholders' money. On reflection, and considered in light of environmental need, it will seem a steadily less ridiculous plan, one that will certainly not lack for detractors at all stages of its development but one that also will in time come to exercise growing appeal to decision-makers and investors throughout the business world.

Rough lines of direction for possible development of such corporately sponsored education need to be sketched, and some of the likely sources of opposition should be pointed out. Beyond this, the environmental benefits of the entire process might be suggested, especially benefits that accrue to man not only as he continues his confrontation with the fragile web of natural life around him but also as he pursues his own human existence as an individual and a social being. The thoughts that follow are an attempt to elaborate on, as well as summarize, these final major points.

Already corporate entities, including those which form subunits of the governmental structure as well as those of private business, are involved in providing various forms of basic education for many categories of employees. Foremen and supervisors attend courses in advanced technical practices, but more important, they can also become involved in activities designed to further their skills in human relations and administration. Executives attend management seminars which, in an atmosphere of mixed practicalism and humanitarianism, deal in wide-ranging probes of managerial techniques and decision-making as these are affected by social and behavioral realities. Opportunities for enlarging one's mental horizon are extended under certain circumstances even to rank-and-file workers, through union- or management-sponsored retreats, optional groups pursuing hobby interests, and the like. Recreational activities under some form of corporate sponsorship are, in fact, perhaps more widespread than the public believes. It would be impossible if even these rather small-scale efforts were not producing some ameliorative and humanizing effects in various levels of employment.

Because corporations are likely to maintain and develop the only secure community structures of the future and are, in comparison to other social institutions, more capable of looking outward and merging their own interests with those of the larger body social, they will find themselves in better position to educate men as individuals and as inhabitants of a complex sociophysical environment. As in every other aspect of life in a mass society, scale plays a vital role in the effectiveness of any agency. Smaller corporations, private or public, are likely to continue to be less able to carry out desirable social-interest functions, especially in such a friction-laden enterprise as that of mass education. Lack of resources is but one reason for this reduced effectiveness of the smaller unit (e.g., regional industry; local or state governments). It will take a long time for such institutions to rid themselves of the folklore and pseudo-independence that carry over from the age of "rugged individualism" and are both the present inspiration for their existence and the token of their future demise. Meantime, they constitute a drag on the forward progress of the larger society. Marginal economically, or in the case of government, not subject to the rationalizations of the actual marketplace, and for the most part functioning in a social vacuum underwritten by adherence to and dependence upon Parkinson's Law, these units will probably tend to disappear long before the question of their reinvesting in significant ways in human capital arises.

The public school district and the private school are special cases in this context. By the nature of their mission, these institutions appear likely to emerge as active participants in the corporate educative process, especially as ways and means can be found to coordinate their work with that of the industrial sector. Meantime, an unnecessary odium remains attached to mass public schooling, a negative evaluation that fails to take into sufficient account the serious limitations of schools in their present relationship to society. Schools cannot achieve large-scale goals of a socially desirable character (e.g., development of environmentally sound behaviors in youth) because they are acting both alone and, given their internal limitations, beyond their scope in setting such goals. "Deschooling" society, however, hardly seems the answer to the problem; integration of school with society in pursuit of a common purpose provides a much more plausible, if not immediately workable, solution. What happens in the adult world of industrial life may yield some clues.

The development of corporate interest in education may manifest itself in a variety of ways. Some of the more obvious possibilities are suggested in what follows. As corporations begin to scour about, cautiously seeking to reinvest profits to maximum effect, newer formulae for reinvestment will arise, modes of expenditure that accept long-term risk along with long-term ambition in the field of social development as prime determinants of policy.[21] Such a new outlook will have become more appropriate, in fact, because of economic trends themselves: profit margins should become established on an ever-more-secure basis, because competition destroys many smaller, less well managed or less well positioned firms once effective in marketing. (Indeed, the whole trend of big business since the end of World War II, if we take American capitalist enterprise as typical, underscores this interpretation: consolidations and diversifications have created a different and in many ways more effective monopolistic structure, which, while it does not allow for greater relaxation of corporate effort in expanding existing markets, does at least permit an earmarking of certain profits on a surer basis over time for purposes not immediately concerned with a corporation's business interests.)

The process under consideration should not be mistaken for the older and more familiar funding of *outside* undertakings of an educative or research nature, usually carried on with monies passed from the capitalist in his philanthropic role, through an intermediary organization, usually a foundation, to persons or groups of a private or institutional character who then carry on their activities wholly separate from the source of original capital. On the contrary, the coming trend seems likely to be for industrial organizations themselves to develop schemes for *internal* activities. As the era of free spending by the great foundations gradually wanes, it will seem only natural for wealth-producing corporations to look for other and more promising approaches to the use of excess profit. The employee-owned industry and the industry that shares profits with its employees are indicators of the future, of a new era in the management of reinvestment funds. The entire redistribution process will more and more be geared to aid individuals in attaining a higher view of themselves as figures in the necessary business of primary production. But to aid individuals in this quest, industry will itself have to yield some part of its dominion over the individual worker: the easiest and most efficient way to do this will be through the complementary action of sharing wealth to make of the individual a figure of greater autonomy and flexibility of behavior.

In the initial phase of corporate involvement in education, the corporation will naturally remain limited in the establishment of its service population. Without doubt its own employees and their families will receive the primary benefits of "first generation" investment in these less tangible "fringe" allocations of excess corporate profit. In this intermediate era all effort will be experimental and tentative, and there will be friction, especially since compulsion to participate, however carefully disguised, cannot at this stage be very well camouflaged in handing out even such innocuous benefits as: prepaid family or individual vacations, which will be taken in certain locales where prearranged combinations of stimuli will attract interest away from self-destructive or environmentally destructive behavior and toward "growth" experiences; increasingly subtle daily *adjunct* experiences in both work and home situations (e.g., novel stimuli woven naturally into the working milieu in such a way that learning cannot be avoided, or home stimulations that unavoidably challenge the individual to participate and learn; the cases of "piped-in" music at work and educational television are only the most innocent forerunner of these adjunct stimulations of tomorrow's communications network); expanded opportunities to engage in direct learning confrontations with a variety of unusual situations, persons, or other stimuli, programmed or not, as *part of the job itself,* confrontations that will demand of the worker continual readjustment and self-renewal.

The importance of individual adaptation to this meteorically shifting reality of the work world of a technologized society has been amply recognized. Tomorrow's technology "requires not men who take orders in unblinking fashion, aware that the price of bread is mechanical submission to authority, but men who can make critical judgments, who can weave their way through novel environments, who are quick to spot new relationships in the rapidly changing reality."[22] Obviously, a great portion of today's humanity, if measured by this requirement, would end on the rubbish heap of history. It is the task of society, through its provision of learning to insure adaptive, environmentally suitable behavior, to bring tomorrow's masses to the point where such requirements can be met.

In the segmented view of society a complaint will at once be registered over the notion that corporations should have a right to enter into competition with formally established schools in providing educational experiences. This is a reaction based solidly in nineteenth-century thinking. It assumes strict functional limitations that apply to any social institution. It stands foursquare against the emerging reality of coalescing individual and group purposes in a society of interdependent, rather than independent, institutions. The point of view espousing strictly limited areas of functioning for each separate institution not only ignores the fact that no single organization can adequately assist the individual to learn all that must be learned in order to adapt successfully; it also reveals a lamentable thought lag inconsistent with the hard truths of an environmental age by showing how much wedded minds are to personal interests and to the unregenerate self as the autistically valid center of the universe.

The presently touted concept of educational accountability is largely based on a view of social and economic institutions as essentially independent entities, or at least entities that do not operate at cross purposes. Certainly in the light of apparent social needs, schools ought to be made to perform more effeciently. But as, say, Jencks's latest work makes clear, equality of educational opportunity is related to factors other than simply provision of formal schooling.[23] Indeed, it is difficult to draw an opposite conclusion even from the educators' standard research work on this subject, that is, the Coleman report.[24] Access to *informal* opportunity for learning, in particular the possibility of participating in less-structured interpersonal experiences in which stimuli likely to alter significantly an individual's perceptions of himself and his future are present, appears to offer the prime means for enhancing *any* learning. If this is true, equality of opportunity for learning and accessibility of learning experiences of a kind favorable to the development of adaptive environmental behavior depend on bridging the gap between formal and informal learning. Accountability then is seen as a common responsibility of all agencies affecting an individual's behavior. But it would be too much to expect that in a transitional society every agency with power to mold a person's behavior would find it possible to see that person as potentially autonomous, seeking freedom to adapt ever more effectively to a situation in which many agencies compete for his commitment. For this reason, only certain agencies at any given moment can exercise in some measure a responsibility for aiding the individual in his search for autonomy through learning. The corporation by virtue of its special hold over employees is able to exercise such a responsibility. Hence, it makes some sense at this stage in history to speak of corporate accountability for individual learning.

One aspect of the communications revolution, that is, its more theoretical potential for affecting mass behavior, has earlier been touched upon. Now the possibilities of this new force in human affairs to affect *individual* behavior must be considered, and specifically in light of the patent need for corporations to take greater responsibility for the learning and behavior of persons who are largely under their physical and psychological control. Communications technology, with its vast capability for producing mass reactions designed to further some business or government interest, can also (as developers of prepackaged educational materials well know) be made to serve the interests of progressive individualization of learning. But this desirable outcome will be attained only on a hit-or-miss basis until some institution within society strong enough to apply the proper stimuli on a continuous and sufficiently personalized basis systematizes the process and makes it available to all its personnel.

Only the corporation, with its unique hold over its workers' lives, can serve this purpose and at the same time monitor the process continuously to make sure that basic goals are being met. Corporations, in their existing infrastructures, easily possess to as great a degree as do more advanced educational institutions the human resources needed to combine the technology of communications and the necessary interpersonal measures by which individual learning will be developed to its maximum potential. They can exert a control over the labor force that no school or college, with their shorter-run educational commitments, can claim. And through the workers, corporations control those other members of society whose opinions today count for a good deal more than was the case even a generation ago — the workers' dependents.

Thus, large corporate entities face a learning future as challenging as that faced by any individual worker. In the environmental epoch, industry's once unitary view of the individual and his social worth must change even as its relationship to society as a whole changes. In this process the corporation will revise its internal policies to accord the worker a status somewhat different from what he enjoyed in the past. Already there are evident signs of a changed worker-employer situation: the corporation will do more for the worker, but the latter must respond in kind by accepting the larger social responsibilities that his new role requires.

The new principle of corporate responsibility, in its turn, involves making available to workers benefits not defined heretofore: intangibles, sources of support over and above the standard "necessaries of life" of the less-imaginative past. The corporation will marshall its complete array of unused resources to stimulate the worker toward self-development. On the level of surface thought, such an operation will, for a long time into the future, seem to many no more than another tired joke of their companies' idea men. But the necessity for this development in the fabric of industrial life will remain and grow in strength, because there is no alternative to it. By means so subtle that they cannot be identified outside the circle of those responsible for their inception, and aided by an equally subtle use of the time element to reinforce those means, industrial man will be thrust forward into unavoidable paths of change and in the process made to slough off his old carapace of negativistic self-rejection. He will be propelled subliminally into a continual, rather than a sporadic, search for learning experiences. The corporate entity will do this to and for the worker, through technology maintained and developed at its own expense — because the price of not doing it would be social disaster, too high a risk to assume.

How Such A System Might Function

Industry will view the idea of formal schooling, in the context of environmental learning, as no more than a starting point. It will recognize that apparently informal learning experiences, where no structure and no element of coercion appear to exist, are superior molders of environmental behavior and the environmental attitude than are formal experiences. Whenever it finds opportunity to develop a worker's existing interest or build a new interest, it will do so; it will never duplicate what established schools have already achieved, since duplication is precisely what needs to be avoided.

Neither will it stop short in its efforts to provide workers with learning opportunities for fear of "invading" the workers' privacy or infringing on individual rights of choice. Given the goals of this kind of corporate activity and given the degree of social need, the question of providing these opportunities becomes largely academic. In present circustances the right of personal choice is invariably and heavily influenced by a whole battery of agencies, ranging from the Madison Avenue advertising establishment, which systematically controls national and international tastes, to the suburban golf club clique, which determines its members' choices in the usual subtle ways associated with strictly local culture groupings. None of these agencies of informal education operates by licence, and it would be absurd to expect corporations to do so either.

A considerable element of pleasurable diversion will of necessity be programmed into this informal learning, but beneath this will lie more serious learning purposes, which gradually the individuals reacting to the imposed learning stimuli will come to recognize and accept as part of "the way things are now." In due course they will demand more, rather than less, of such mediated learning experiences. As workers see the benefits to themselves of unhindered access to such secondary "occupations," which can both hold their interest and keep them on the path of environmentally constructive behavior, they will in some degree accept even the reduction of old-time uninhibited, individualistic pursuits with good grace. Their attention will direct itself somewhat more toward the mental tasks that the new informal learning will stimulate, and somewhat away from the present ubiquitous preoccupation with behavior directed toward social and commercial goals. This development will, of course, have serious consequences for business concerns founded and operated solely on the principle of endless consumption and endless growth in material things or on the principle of standard group reaction to cultural stimuli (e.g., the existing entertainment industries).

Electronic communications technology today already possesses a theoretical capability for making possible direct mental contact between any two persons on earth. But the manner in which this technology is controlled serves to channel the rapidly increasing flow of communications so as to preserve the preexisting web of expectations and predictable effects. This capability will in due time be sufficiently realized in practice so as to permit continuous exchange of data and opinion, directly and instantaneously or via idea banks. The number of information "sythesists" and idea bearers is even now in the process of expanding enormously. The impulse to become part of such a charmed circle, noticeable as it has already become in intellectual and managerial classes, will stir into life the latent intellectualism of the better-endowed workers, with reinforcing effects upon them by then semi-developed organizations of informal learning sponsored by the corporations.

As exploration of the social uses of advanced communications capabilities progresses, it is likely that changes will be forced in the policies of media systems formerly relying on exploitation of a few formulae of entertainment and a handful of established personalities. With an audience better educated and more demanding than any hitherto in existence, all programming becomes more difficult. Problems of this kind are even at this early stage being wrestled with by television corporations and other mass media. Here, too, corporate efforts at informal education can exercise important effects on reader and viewer reactions. But even in advance of this development it is significant to note that the role of the media, in promoting substantive, popular reactions to Vietnam and Watergate has on a large scale among the American people been at least in part directed against the *withholding* of information. The public itself in America has "the conviction that neither the state, nor special-interest groups, nor institutions — however praiseworthy their goals — nor industry, nor the army, nor anyone or anything else has the right to refuse to explain its actions or to withhold information."[25] Any attempt to stop information flow in so modern a society is no longer passed by without notice. This information flow lies at the heart of an environmentalized social order and the censor or clique maintaining a secret decision-making process will bear tomorrow's social obloquy. Corporations, whatever their products, cannot afford a negative public image; they will move with all deliberate swiftness to enhance rather than stifle information flow. They will accept their new task as social educators.

This emphasis on the availability of information indeed requires a strong base in society's more viable institutions. The exchange of critical information among different institutions is neccessary in order to prevent, among other ills, the building up of status cliques, "experts" and specialists who attempt to resist change rather than support it, by propagating myths of indispensability and by creating networks of agents or functionaries whose existence cannot be justified in environmental cost-accountability terms. The interdependence of persons will be matched by the interdependence of institutions. Freedom of information will act to integrate the hitherto separate functions of institutions with presumably specialized goals. Without this openness, the coming advances in technology (e.g., nearly all products for human use, save food, will come to exist through recycling; nearly all human energy needs will be provided from solar sources) are likely to prove meaningless. What will these accomplishments signify, if they are not paralleled by advances in human interpersonal behavior consonant with the interests of a people living sanely in an environmental age?

Within the corporation informal, interpersonal educative contacts have already been carried on for generations, it may be noted, but such activity has generally been limited to top-echelon experts or the less culturally hidebound, middle-rung technicians to whom the accidents of propinquity have yielded natural opportunities for learning. Today, as we reap some of the benefits of continued and stepped-up formal education extending back over the schooling careers of the last few generations, we find a higher percentage of the populace potentially capable of profiting from broader learning opportuntities. Such opportunities, however, are typically lacking in home and work environments.

In its initial moves toward the establishment of corporate responsibility for providing these opportunities, the industrial leadership will proceed formally. While this is necessary as an opening wedge, it cannot of course guarantee results. It is a measure of corporate weakness as well as lack of imagination. Yet, as a recognition of the workers' needs, it will exercise a helpful function in group psychology. In any case, we may assume that this formal acknowledgment of responsibility will come when management appoints an education officer for the firm.

But the mere appointment of such an individual cannot of itself bring on a new phase in social-industrial evolution. It is barely a beginning. The working out of a whole network of educative contacts within the corporate structure could be attempted on paper and even formally proclaimed. But this would be meaningless until there developed a ground swell of rank-and-file effort to make corporate educational development a reality.

To date, the relative simplicity of communications policy and technological implementation have mandated a pedestrian rate of development of radical and qualitatively diverse interpersonal learning. As yet what has been typical still remains typical. Ranting radio preachers, repetitious television emcees, cantankerous newpaper columnists, and others of this ilk continue to dominate the substantive exchanges of information that keep society moving at its generally prosaic intellectual level. Today's student class is the wave of the future. As never before, speaking in terms of sheer numbers, youth seeks a relationship, either personally or through print, with a relative handful of master thinkers who are the inheritors and preservers of a tradition of elitist learning. There is an inherent contradiction in such a relationship, for this youth is perforce the vanguard of a *mass* tradition; what makes the relationship valid, however, is the common search for a key to knowledge over and above the outdated shibboleths of yesterday's structured society. Objectivism is the common ground of both the old elitists and the youthful mass environmentalists. At this stage their essentially different commitments do not interfere with their marriage of convenience. The interim arrangement also helps to cloud temporarily the need of the youthful environmental thinkers to establish once and for all their permanent alliance with the industrial workers.

Communications developments of the fairly near future seem likely to change all this. Youth will see its opportunities to establish itself as a force for betterment within the industrial infrastructure much widened and will use the new communications systems to identify itself with the objects of its communication, that is, the workers. Future Peace Corps "junkets" will not involve sending young people to Africa or Brazil. The young will, instead, bring their enthusiasms and strong urges for learning (and their ignorance as well) into the industrial system itself. They will communicate there and be communicated with. This development too will be but another facet in the growth of an interpersonal communications network, a network designed to draw men into that rarefied dimension of human experience called learning. This is part of the overall social attack on ignorance, and it is environmental to the core. It seeks an ideal, the ideal of balance — within and without, in the individual psyche and between that psyche and the universe that pulsates everywhere outside the body housing it.

It must be admitted that all this is predicated upon as yet highly fragile assumptions: that learning, even in the best of circumstances, must still be sought by the individual, that it cannot be forced on him; and, even more uncertain, that society will not break down under the violent buffetings of continual change before a system can be imposed that will permit this radical extension of learning opportunity. Least certain of all, one cannot fully trust the endurance of the human body. The energy needs for any individual's successful functioning through the treacherous near future are enormous; assumed is a physical capability that, it cannot be denied, may not exist. Wild-eyed educators who have swallowed the systems analysis principle whole are neglecting to consider the possible physical limitation on man's potential for receiving learning stimuli.

> The process of image formation and classification is, in the end, a physical process, dependent upon finite characteristics of nerve cells and body chemicals. In the neural system as now constituted there are, in all likelihood, inherent limits to the amount and speed of image processing that the individual can accomplish. How fast and how continuously can the individual revise his inner images before he smashes up against these limits?"[26]

Yet, if one cannot predicate man's continued ability to resist the physical deterioration that excessive change is capable of working upon him, he has in essence given up the future of man in the universe, an outcome alien to human thinking by both tradition and the whole value system that the socialized individual is wont to cultivate in his interpersonal behavior. It is possible that the race may descend, worldwide, to the level of hatred and lovelessness that characterizes, in Colin Turnbull's trenchant and poignant description, one remote, diminishing tribe of black Africans.[27] But as long as the mass of men think in terms of some kind of progress and self-development, plans for and visions of the future will prevail. Under the goad of environmental needs, the concept of corporate involvement in education on a constantly expanding scale should come to seem far less than radical to the thinking person's mind.

What is perhaps most difficult about the whole proposition of extending education into the life of every worker is its undeniable *mass* aspect. Nothing of this kind has been attempted before and even now the very idea of such a development is still reacted to with sarcasm or disbelief. Yet the absolute social broadening of the conditions of existence will constitute the effective completion of the next stage, the environmentalizing step, in man's evolution. If the movement does not affect a significant portion of industrialized humanity in the time available, failure may be reliably assumed. It hardly seems possible that without full support of socioeconomic power centers (the various corporate establishments, in all their variety) can mankind take that necessary leap — out of the disillusion of today and into the dizzying new land of revealed socioenvironmental truth, the land of the twenty-first century.

It should not be thought that at this point experience in linking educational pursuits and industrial labor is entirely lacking. Since 1906 the system known as "cooperative education" has been in operation in industrial regions of the United States. It is a formal, jointly sponsored college program in which "work experience constitutes a regular and essential element in the educative process and some minimum standards of successful performance on the job are included in the requirements of the institution for a degree."[28] This program has some pertinence to developments over the horizon in corporate sponsorship of learning activities, but its limitations should be clearly perceived: a) it is a cooperative system, true, but it remains *formal,* a credit-counting concept of education; b) it gives the college-age student practical work experience to supplement his classroom and other academic experiences; it does *not* assist the fully employed individual to supplement his work experience with broadening learning activities.

Broadening learning activities must gradually become the focus of major development under sponsorship of a convinced corporate leadership, but many early steps will involve a painful amount of trial and error. Some vanguard firms, still obsessed with older ideals of the management process even as they recognize the new direction toward company involvement in worker welfare, will probably import a corps of educationists to fill important-sounding but substantively pointless positions, men and women who may be expected to labor over the usual academic paperwork without bringing into being any change worth noting. This would be typical, perhaps, of a point of view, at both leadership and change-agent levels, that automatically identifies evident expenditure of effort, rather than evident results, with progress. But the beginnings of a genuine movement for change may lie in this direction as well as another.

Attitude change among industrial rank-and-file seems likely to follow rather than precede change in two other spheres: a) in the improvement of mechanical communications systems and their increasing ability to respond flexibly to individuals' needs and wants; b) in revising and making more socially responsive the organizational structure of the corporation itself. The technical gains of computer science and allied fields should in due time allow for the development of much more extensive use of the man-machine interface. A worker on an assembly line, for example, who needs to spend only short periods of time actually fully involved with his job and has minutes-long interuptions between periods, can be provided with a television monitor and headphones, so that during his free time a programmed, educational, diverting series of audiovisual experinces specifically *tied in to the continuity of his work,* linking job-related and job-unrelated perceptions in a single flow, would be beamed to him. Thus mechanical and psychological scientists will combine forces to produce a whole range of devices into which developmental stimuli will be programmed, as sensory data, to individualize, wholly without pain, psychologically and temporally apt learning experiences. Naturally, the negatively conditioned worker in the first generation or two of such machines will look upon them as something of a joke. Later, with increasing sophistication, these providers of diverting and self-reinforcing mental experience will become a matter of course, accepted as part of one's way of life. People will come to interest themselves in such means of assisting self-development for yet another reason: the social and, indeed, environmental gains to behavior will by then have become obvious to everyone.

Industry will fill the role of supplier and developer of this mechanical spur to workers' self-development. It will recognize the value of the machine as a superior motivator, because the machine can individualize stimuli to so much greater a degree than can a human and for a lower cost. But industry will also recognize the need of any worker for both significant human contact in the work situation and for identifying himself with a humanized hierarchy within the industry itself. This will not only require "bosses" who are of an exceptional approachability and degree of understanding, a development that cannot be avoided, but also mean changes in the entire communications philosphy of the corporation.

The vertical communications channel, the chain-of-command principle, is vital to any corporate structure and cannot, of course, be tampered with in relation to the orderly process of decision-making. But when one begins to intrude upon this formal structure an informal educational undertaking, some informality and flexibility will naturally find their way into the operation. Decentralization and diffusion of responsibility are the reinforcers of such an educational commitment. They "fit in" with the accent on individualized experience. With employee welfare and psychic betterment a corporate responsibility, communications down through the chain of command can emphasize in less formal ways the human side of industrial life.

To be sure, busy executives will have no more time then

than now for useless chit-chat. The specific managerial
function of an executive, as laid down in his job description,
will, however, always permit of amplification in its human
relations aspect. Today's ironclad vertical system of administration can and will be altered to promote various new modes
of communication, outside the formal decision-making and
protocol responsibilities. Lateral and diagonal communications contacts within a corporate infrastructure can be
expanded and, through a computerized system similar to
that already in commercial use to arrange "computer dating,"
bring together persons with like or coinciding nonwork interests. While the point could easily be overstressed, certain
changes in the basic on-line production system in heavy
industry (e.g., the "team" approach to replace assembly-line
production in which each worker performs one, and only
one, function, continuously, an approach now being used by
the Volvo auto company in Sweden) already point to a trend
toward a "varied-experience" format as the basis of any
worker's industrial life. By extension, this development
within the production process itself can easily apply to the
educational aspect of corporate existence. Many further
changes and variations in the working milieu to reach such
goals may be expected.

Thus, opportunities are gradually emerging; they suggest
an infinitude of resources that can ultimately be applied to
the fulfillment of the individual's psychic and educational
needs even while he engages in a legitimate occupation.
Individualization of these opportunities will take a corresponding infinite variety of methods. While informal learning
directed toward social and personal development will be the
goal of any corporate program, the worker's own choice
must prevail. In that choice he will be aided by others, but
neither dictated to nor hurried. He will have difficulty
knowing how to proceed, because of the range of resources
of which he can make use. He may spend years in nothing
more than an extended sampling process. Or he may, at the

opposite extreme, elect to formalize his learning experience to a great degree.

No matter what particular path or arrangement may be chosen, a technology and supporting human services will assist. Telecommunications systems exist such as those developed by AT&T, which utilize multi-media information retrieval, dial access, and other machine processes that permit bypassing the usual printed-matter systems of learning, and promise information dispersal and resource availability for any user and to any purpose. The hardware aspect can hardly develop other than in advance of actual need, of course. Motivational, organizational, and developmental issues remain the more serious concern.

In this regard, the essential difficulty continues to be that of extending the understanding of the needs of persons working at various levels and under various psychological restraints within the corporation to those in a position to effect change. The process is one of improved and directed communications, as has been pointed out. There is inevitable in all this an implicit broadening of democratization within the firm. Individualization of work assignments, despecialization, the greater integration of worker and corporate interests — these straws in the wind suggest an eventual alteration in the monolithic character of the corporation. The point at which communications capabilitites and trust will have so built up the sense of group solidarity that management everywhere cedes its mania for unquestioned authority and establishes as policy a broader-based decision-making process will also be the point at which environmentalism enters social life in its substantive form.

It would be premature to suggest that this millennium is in sight or even just over the horizon. But already on the upper and middle levels of corporate infrastructures lateral communications, expanded in the normal course of business evolution, must have beneficial spin-off effects in the interpersonal and group domains of informal learning. In the academic world one surprising and continuing innovation in the decision-making function seems to bespeak an enlargement of the principle of shared authority which, if followed to its natural limits, must inevitably lead to representation of broader interests in all management decisions and a fellowship of different status levels in a learning atmosphere, namely, the inclusion of students on college and university selection committees. Such a development may bear an even broader connotation: that society will sooner or later force changes in man's views of the profit principle itself; that the concept of efficiency lies more in sharing than getting; that humanity can make better use of the talents of those who today in both the West and the East shun and divest themselves of the gentler virtues to espouse corporate exclusivism and the all-governing rules of behavior of the marketplace philosophy.

Some word of caution now seems in order. What has been said to this point must be seen in perspective. Progress in human society has never been automatic, nor will it be even in the world of 2,000, although those who have not reflected sufficently on the human cost of past progress, and the complications for any enterprise of unlooked-for human perversities, may take it rather too much for granted. We face a critical period of adjustment in global society, without stable guidelines in politics, economics, or the necessary counterpart to technological advance, which has been tentatively labeled "social engineering." We are entering, with little preparation, that gray, in-between world marked, in Drucker's terminology, by the "end of continuity,"[29] or by what Michael describes as chaos in the midst of order and world "complexity" and "turmoil."[30]

The malleability of the human material undergoing such experiences of change, with heavy demands upon human powers of self-control and nervous endurance, can hardly be assumed automatically. Internalization by the masses of norms of behavior suitable to a futurist society, since it requires *remaking* significant patterns of present behavior, becomes a radical and evolutionary undertaking. This cannot be accomplished without a conscious effort by all those forces of society capable of exerting the necessary pressures. And those forces must be made to work together. Leadership and innovation must be assumed at the proper time and by the right parties. Industry cannot escape its role in this undertaking.

Transformation of the adult work environment in the direction of human self-development is the single, most-needed initial innovation of a changeover era. The first employer to offer full pay for eight hours of work while his employee spends seven of those hours on the job and one hour in self-chosen, genuinely educative pursuits will have taken a giant step toward the futurist world. From this model foothold, transformation of every stage of the work process can be undertaken with greater ease and assurance. Too, transformation of other, less socially and economically autonomous institutions (schools, clubs, the family itself) becomes both more feasible and more necessary. The older notions of discrete institutional functions should, over a span of generations, die out because they do not accord well enough with the needs of an integrated society of self-directed individuals.

To combat the social and psychological problems of the near future and to overcome them, more genuinely adaptive behavior is required. Man has no choice other than to learn such behavior and to use it. This is the root process involved in environmental learning. No one can say that maladaptation will have been conquered simply when fewer crimes are committed or when statistics show that more people as a percentage of the population are given over to nondisruptive acts. One cannot logically hold that society has the right to eradicate this last vestige of the old free-wheeling individualism from the spectrum of behavior by, so to speak, psychological bullying. But one *can* with justification, in light of our knowledge of environmental imperatives, seek to hasten the day when all the brunt of personal and group passions is more directly susceptible of humane control. This is another way of stating what the environmental ethic says to humanity: when social institutions give evidence to the average intelligent human being that his personal life goals are not incompatible with their goals, or vice-versa, then a truly environmentalized social order will have come to exist.

4

Learning Emphasis in an Environmental Age: The New Meaning of a General Education

The specialist is a person of whom today's society has a real, even an obvious, need. He invents complicated machines and then, equally important, makes them run properly. He can explain troublesome mysteries of many kinds, scientific, social, behavioral, even philosophical. He has become an essential cog in our complex business of making society run and, to make the ultimate admission, he acts as the basic cutting edge in man's eternal struggle for knowledge. He may also be the man of whom Nietzsche spoke in the following terms: "A specialist . . . begins to resemble nothing but a factory workman who spends his whole life in turning one particular screw or handle on a certain instrument or machine."[1]

Higher education has wrestled with the problem of balance between general and specialized education for a very long time. Its solutions, by and large, have been compromises worked out in the larger context of institutional imperatives. There is abiding uncertainty that in their claims for "individualized" learning colleges and universities may mistake the

87

individual's ability to make his own relatively free choice
between generalizing and specializing in his program of study.
What really are the relative merits of the two when one
tries to project a reasonably accurate view of today's college
student as he will look twenty or twenty-five years later?
Even so establishment-oriented a critic as Woodring pauses
to wonder over what a formal education for short-term needs
will do for (or *to*) a person in terms of his total career.[2] Yet
one has to be, as the commonplace phrase has it, realistic.
The first-time employment-seeker poring over job descriptions
is made to realize that the need for skills of a more general
nature or capabilities for integration, except for some few
highly professional occupations, are in the final analysis of
secondary importance. Technical specializing stands with
intimidating restraint as a *sine qua non* for job entry almost
ubiquitously in a post-industrial society. This accounts, not
surprisingly, for the widespread suspicion that "know-how,"
the so-called specialist expertise, is more an invention of
controlling bureaucracies than an actual need in job performance, particularly when one becomes familiar with the
actual specifics of a given position.[3]

Another aspect of the age-old dichotomy of the general
versus the special is the extent to which its existence widens
and reinforces the generation gap. Access to positions of
control or influence over policy affairs universally presupposes
steady progression upward on the career ladder. The career
ladder itself is suspect, indeed, since from the importance
placed upon it a further suspicion arises, namely, that age and
experience are falsely enthroned as the only advance guaran-
tors to employers of successful job performance. Any general
learning acquired prior to initial entry into the labor market
thus loses its meaningfulness, save as a sentimental exercise
in a self-development that comes too early and does too
little for the individual's sense of future security. There is a
legitimate sense of frustration in today's youth; it stems not
only from the inability to savor education in breadth at a
time when inexperience works heavily against getting genuine

satisfaction out of such a form of learning, but also from natural distrust, when youth finds itself bound too soon to what it sees as unfulfilling, confining specialization and a resultant inability to develop a perspective on more valuable and lasting goals of living.

A New View: Using General and Specialized Knowledge

In a significant degree the environmental ethos appears to allow a readier approach to this problem. This should become even more the case after the passage of another decade or so, when the demand for specialists in the narrow sense seems likely to fall off and the technologically advanced society gives itself a breathing space in which to restudy the problem of human occupations and the relation of that problem to providing mass education. Meantime, it might be well to keep in mind, in this connection, the phenomenon of a possible breakdown in the supply-demand system as it operates with respect to highly trained specialists. Not only did the first Nixon administration, for example, witness the much-discussed, government-generated cancellation of thousands of specialist jobs in the aerospace industry but this administration also witnessed the startling turnabout of supply-demand factors in teaching, the nation's largest profession, creating a huge surplus of highly trained professionals in education — part of the festering sore of unemployment that helps maintain the American figure on unemployment at or above a socially unacceptable five percent.[4] It would be well to ponder the extent to which a consumer society like that of contemporary America might respond, if and when its supposedly self-correcting economic system again entered a decline comparable to that of the Depression, with millions (including a high percentage of professionals) unemployed, and might respond with such violence that the racial outbursts of the late 1960s in America's major cities would pale by comparison.

It must be granted that nothing could be more futile than

trying to disparage *all* forms of specialized training and at the same time to praise to the skies anything that can be lumped under the heading of a liberal education. For one thing, the categories tend regularly to blur. No one can specify where, precisely, in an ongoing experience of learning, the specialized education leaves off and the general (usually considered as hardly distinct from a "liberal" education) begins, or vice-versa. Also, it is not hard to admit that both general and specialized education can bore the learner as easily as inspire him; there are no advance guarantees in any part of the learning process.

Discussion at many levels of the American educational system regarding "career education" has had the beneficial effect of bringing renewed attention to the distinction between the "cash-value" and the intangible goals of any education. In this difficult world a reasonably useful but less specialized preparation, it would seem, might prove the most sensible alternative for many youth dissatisfied with the prospect of making their way in a blatantly competitive professional field that prevents the cultivation of outside interests. The complexity of young peoples' problems in making early career decisions should, however, warrant some mild expression of distrust at the highly optimistic approaches of certain spokesmen for "career education":

> Ideally, career education should help every student find and prepare for a rewarding occupation, whether he leaves high school without a diploma or graduates from college. Even falling short of the ideal, which most human enterprises tend to do, career education by the very nature of its emphasis should help many more young people find their way into productive, satisfying employment than is now the case.[5]

In any case, ways and means to maximum adaptation through any educational experience ought not to be overlooked, and the exact "mix" of special and general education in any given case should be viewed in the context of environmental ideals. We ought not to misunderstand, for one thing, what a general (as opposed to a specialized) education involves today. In the more hidebound spirit of old-time liberal education, extending from the Greeks to Maritain and Hutchins, a trend toward the advance specification of what knowledge was appropriate for general education has dominated every curriculum. We are here led to conceive of a full general education as consisting only of certain fixed subject matters, dealt out to successive generations of learners unchanged in their essentials but varied in their presentation to accord with individual needs and ability levels as perceived at given moments in time. This kind of education is general by verbal definition only, to the extent that it equates education with an acquaintance with the "great books." Environmentally speaking, however, general education should equate with general experience. It is an education not often met with in schools and colleges, because the latter are too bound up with the codification and regurgitation of bits and pieces of subject matter to be able to bring the tyro at learning to an integration of his experience.[6]

Specialized knowledge, broadly speaking, can be attained by anyone. It is available or discoverable information, as well as the developed ability to use it in some essentially practical way. A good many practitioners in various professions, to be sure, especially salaried people dependent upon the whim of an employer for the maintenance of their jobs, will claim more than this: that *only* a professional person who has come up through the ranks can both acquire this knowledge and use it in a socially beneficial way. The problem of specialization and the professions can hardly concern us here in any detail. The sole point to be made is that the data of specialized knowledge are of themselves objective and public. Specialized knowledge is limited to a small clique of inner circle savants only because the conditions of the lives of the mass of men prevent their acquaintance with it. Theoretically, any human being with the power to learn in an organized way could attain a working knowledge of the body of learning within a discipline or specialized field.

General knowledge, at least in the environmental sense, differs from specialized knowledge in that it represents what the individual does with what he learns and how he comes to view himself in a universal environment. This does not mean that it begins merely where the specialized education leaves off. It is not simply a matter of integration within a single brain of various bits of subject matter having some common relationships. It is literally the personification of experience, what *makes* the individual what he is and gives him the sense (whether acquired as a by-product of academic study or through other means) of his own identity in the universe. This difficult concept was perhaps best expressed by Whitehead when he wrote:

> What we should aim at producing is men who possess both culture and expert knowledge in some special direction. Their expert knowledge will give them the ground to start from, and their culture will lead them as deep as philosophy and as high as art. We have to remember that the valuable intellectual development is self-development.[7]

The average teacher, unfortunately, has not only not pondered this distinction; he has not come even close to understanding its significance for modern man. This means that the procedures used by most teachers to communicate their knowledge are too inflexible to make learning meaningful in the sense of general education.

> The teaching procedure we are looking for must be one which will apply to children in *physical* groups, since that is the way they are found in the school, without treating them simultaneously as *psychological or social* groups. That is, it must be a pedagogy which can rise above the physical sociality of the classroom to affirm the psychic identity of each of the several human beings located there.[8]

The failure to date to provide this affirmation of individual psychic identity has been a measure of the school's failure in society. Some recent research efforts have been made to apply a comprehensive theory of personality organization to the teaching act as it affects the learning process and/or learning outcomes.[9] Little of a positive nature can be gleaned from these efforts thus far, but it does seem clear that a general education (again in the environmental sense) depends far more upon personality interactions and psychic factors, at least as these come to bear in formal learning situations, than upon a learner's ability to progress in the accumulation of specified quantities of discrete items of specialized knowledge.

Even so, it is obvious that a general education *must* consist of more than giving an individual a sense of himself, which can be defined to encompass any animal or autistic *amourpropre,* however trivial. There must also be present as broad an acquaintance as possible with the data and value alternatives presented by the world of events and physical forms. Beyond this, the learner in an environmental age would also be expected to derive from a general education a point of view toward the outside world that is at one and the same time idiosyncratic, flexible, and realistic, that gives a basis for comprehending his own and his environment's limitations as they are placed in unavoidable juxtaposition. When this kind of education, for this point of view, emerges from formal school learning, then we can begin to speak of having engineered an environmental education — one, incidentally, that is also a general education in the completest contemporary sense. Lacking this, we have to remain content with what most people now have: not an environmental and a general education but a mere compound of undigested bits of objective information and unfocused emotional reactions. Consideration of the extent of mass ignorance in today's world, even in the advanced societies, should remind one of how far indeed the race has to travel, educationally speaking, and in how short a time.

Its tragic incompleteness is, in fact, the chief hallmark of much of human education, if by completeness we mean the attainment through accumulated learning experiences of the personal power by which to reinforce and redirect the self in the business of adaptive living. Something of the blame for incomplete education can be laid to the schools and to the short-sightedness of those elements in society which control or influence formal education. But society as a whole has to bear its own share of responsibility for a situation in which too many citizens have not as children learned even the beginnings of behavioral self-sufficiency, with the result that as adults their struggles to cope with change and challenge lead to endlessly recurrent ineffectual outcomes, helping neither themselves nor society.

While the need for a general education with adaptive focus spreads through all layers of the social order, serious problems arise when one attempts to prescribe specific educational applications designed to bring such an education to all and sundry. No one person can meet the demands for ongoing adaptation to a complex milieu by being taught, trained, conditioned, or exposed to the same set of experiences as another person. Again the stern challenge of individualization presents itself. The individual must be allowed to retain and develop his own psychic identity even while through his educational experience he attains a better grasp of the systematized nature of knowledge and of the necessary self-discipline that will reflect itself in environmentally suitable behavior. We can perhaps better see the difficulties of this task if we consider briefly one of the most highly touted current-day overviews of how the formal process of learning can be maximized, and do so in the context, just developed, of a general environmental education.

Behavioral Objectives:
Two Divergent Approaches

In recent years the term *behavioral objectives* has become nearly synonymous with the systematization of school learning. The high priests of this movement[10] declare that there are "obvious differences between statements of objectives that are ambiguous, and true *definitions* of objectives, which are not."[11] In essence, since being wholly specific about one's objectives is the one great necessity, one must limit learning processes to those situations which allow for exercise of judgment by an observer who, without bias and with total objectivity, can state following a learner's response that it either does or does not meet the established learning criterion.

One behavioral definition of a learning objective is "a verbal statement that communicates reliably to any individual (who knows the words of the statement as concepts) *the set of circumstances that identifies a class of human performances.*"[12] Certainly there exists in this construct an admirable intention, namely, that with reference to any verifiable exercise in learning we must specify a *performance* that exemplifies the learning in an *action,* one observable by any intellectually competent person. The extreme clarity of this prescription has, naturally, caused most students of the learning process to line up on one side or the other of an argument that has now raged for the better part of a decade.[13]

It is interesting to note that on one point all parties to the dispute agree: there must be educational objectives. The extent of agreement tends to carry even farther, in fact, with a general acceptance that the teacher bears prime responsibility for deciding which objectives will be specified. A spokesman for the anti-behavioral objectives faction, for example, states that "it is not the schools but the teachers who must decide what objectives should be specified, and they must do so as individuals, taking their students into consideration. They must therefore acquire the knowledge and skills that are needed to specify educational objectives and evaluate the results obtained. Behavioral objectivists can help by providing models to spur investigation."[14]

The whole issue, in both its theoretical and practical aspects, can take on a more positive cast when viewed from the standpoint of environmental philosophy. This philosophy, based in behavioral realism, would seek answers to certain questions that, to the limited human mind, involve a heavy load of contradictions: Can the specified objectives be applied to the education of individuals and made use of effectively, while at the same time preserving each individual's status as a unique person with unique creature needs? Can a system that has such explicit behavioral aims and limitations do man a genuine service (assuming that the ideals of both its detractors and its supporters were combined into a more effective synthesis than one encounters today), a service by which learning how to behave in a world of rapid change and intimidating controls can actually be enhanced? Naturally, no one claims behavioral objectives as the solution to *every* problem. Otherwise, however, the answers to these difficult questions would seem to be a guarded yes — *if* educational science can develop learning structures appropriate to every individual's absolute uniqueness in learning and behavior.

Any theory of learned behavior, if that behavior is sub-stantially related to social life, suggests behavioral objectives of some kind. What limits one places on the objectives will depend on one's use for the behavior in question. For the environmental thinker, single-instance behavior has no meaning out of context. Only the basic directions of an organism's behavior have ultimate significance. The argument of the anti-behavioral-objectives group in one major aspect is that the behavioral-objective approach to instruction "rests on assumptions about human behavior that are reduc-tionist, deterministic, and physicalist. It is opposed to the view that learning is self-directed, unstructured, and in large part unpredictable."[15] In this criticism one can grasp some-thing of the either-or character of a debate that has, because moral social behavior is not accepted by either side as the ultimate basis of learning, deteriorated into something of a verbal slugging match between those who espouse a freer, liberal educational philosophy and the scientifically possessed educational technologists who are determined to systematize and regulate learning in its every aspect.

The objective of any learning process requires some expectation of performance, some measurable behavior to show that the learning process has been effective. But so long as performance criteria cannot be specified precisely, doubt will exist as to whether or not the objective has been reached. And decidedly, from the environmental point of view, reduction to "just one thing" of the objective, in order to minimize vagueness about what specifics are to be included in the test performance, amounts to a patent negation of the many-sidedness of behavioral experience as we know it today. Yet even when a fairly acceptable, presumably relevant combination of objective and criterion performance has been achieved (e.g., the learner will give at an appropriate point in the eighth-grade ecology course an explanation of how the water cycle affects various living organisms, with examples provided from x number of categories in the plant kingdom and x number in the animal kingdom), even given this statement of the objective and the criterion performance and assuming a performance complete from either the determinist or the broad-field standpoint, the teacher can still only with rash overconfidence claim to have fulfilled his entire function. In the sense of environmental completeness, the standard behavioral objectives debate at this juncture seems to break down on both sides. Consider this question: How does the learner's performance, although successfully carried out at this stage of learning, relate to an optimum continuity of knowledge to be developed through later time, and what range of behaviors does a teacher hypothesize for a future period of time, to give evidence that the learner is using all his capabilities in the development of an adaptive self?

The questions cannot begin to be answered with any precision in the present state of the instructional art. Many specialists in education, in fact, steeped in their particular parochial approach to learning, steadfastly refuse to be drawn out into the general field where such a question can be considered. The knowledge industry, having packaged knowledge in so-and-so many airtight compartments, finds itself at a loss in facing up to the staggering generality of that philosophical issue which underlies the behavioral objectives controversy. To admit how much importance is attached to a philosophical outlook in the educational enterprise would be to admit how petty, although necessary, specialization for its own sake has tended to become. Everyone hates to belittle his own means of livelihood. Yet value problems must be faced. An environmental era demands a kind of learning suited to optimum human development under conditions of growing stress and complexity. Only general learning can meet these new needs, a general *environmental* learning that creates a person whose behavior transcends all the narrow bounds of specialization.

This imperative, while it clarifies the aims of formal education, also brings about problems, since it poses a new and trenchant challenge to vested interests in formal education. It must by its very nature threaten those elements in the tradition of formal education which are obsolescent and retrograde. Specifically, it signals the long-overdue breakdown of the specialized subject-matter interests, with their basis in a social-occupational rationale less and less suited to the emerging needs of environmentalized humanity. Perhaps, even without the goad of an onrushing environmental movement, given its intimate identification with specialization and specialized motives in the old social order, subject matter as the sole determining factor in the organization of learning would take on a suspect character. But the environmental cause has inevitably hurried recognition of the insufficiency of a single-minded approach to the business of public education.

The obviously intense need for adaptive education rather than a dull repetition, generation after generation, of mere stored-up data mistakenly taken for useful or relevant knowledge has been recognized by the mass society itself in its criticisms of formal, traditional education. The next move is up to the educational leadership. It is patently necessary at this point to look beyond the single subjects themselves, beyond career education, even beyond the various novel, experimental, cross-disciplinary efforts of a handful of imaginative forerunners in the planning of learning experiences. In the era of socioenvironmentally adaptive behavior, it will be impossible to divert indefinitely to other fields the resources needed to engineer suitable learning opportunities for a mass society. The scope of this necessary undertaking will have to be recognized, and, hopefully, recognized before all lead time has elapsed and we find ourselves embarked on a project for which little or no advance planning has been done — a project that must involve labor of incredible proportions, not all of which by any means can be done by machines. For achievement of environmental general learning in tomorrow's advanced society will be, for its time, what the Pyramids, the Great Wall of China, and the cathedrals of Europe were in theirs.

Toward an Environmental General Education

So then, if not merely subject matter and then more subject matter, what will provide the basis of this new, this adaptive general education? Surely it will not be unadulterated career emphasis, for this would merely repeat, at a lower level of intellectual sophistication, the errors of Ph.D. or even more highly specialized technical education. And just as surely, it cannot be an emphasis on simulations or "playing at the problems of real life," for this approach will in too many cases end as no more than a glorified and extended sensitivity training, a make-believe exercise, the limitations of which must become apparent to all but those few who have something personal to gain from it. Surely, too, it will not be an emphasis on everyone's "doing his own thing," for this popular and mistakenly approved denial of the worth of both group processes and the traditions of human interpersonal experience negates the very value basis of the indivudualization being sought.

An answer to this question at the present time would seem

to lie in the principle of balance in the humanistic use of educational diagnosis and follow-up to serve the individual-social development of the person. When this rock-bottom principle is combined with the theoretical potential of a rapidly developing computer science, a picture, however vague as yet, of future posibilities begins to emerge. Against this educational and scientific rationale, with the assumption of constant new breakthroughs in the technological support system, the chief components of educational experience — subject matter, introspection, simulations, dialectic, inter-actions, "real life" occurrences — can be worked, however roughly, into individual patterns to accord in increasing measure with individual and social needs.[16]

It will doubtless be argued, in the same cynical language that is applied to other ideas whose time has not yet arrived (e.g., the behavior modification concepts of B. F. Skinner), that this approach must necessarily founder against the operating tenets of democracy, that it can end only by "programming" the individual and denying essential rights and freedoms. In answer to this across-the-board criticism, one can express partial, though unequivocal, agreement: such an education *will* tend to deny every individual the freedom to learn and perform those acts which are likely to bring on additional friction between him and society, but it will do this in a way that should actually make him prefer the education so offered and the behavior he will subsequently carry out. This is not only a reasonable but a necessary next step in the global task of rationalizing social resources humanely. It also serves the interest of preserving a basic minimum of social control in societies subject to ever-increasing pressures for equalization in accessibility to resources and life opportunities.

Nevertheless, the emphasis remains on individualization. This general education for environmental living will be first and last an individualized learning, if only because it must be in order to preserve the individual as an indestructible core of humane thinking and behavior. Communist China and the

U.S.S.R. give evidence of having reduced observable internal friction in their societies to a considerable degree, but they have done so by main force or psychological threat. This means that on a mass basis the individual's right to freely shape his own thought and behavior has been seriously eroded and that the individual possesses no autonomy beyond that provided by his identification with the state. In the successful societies of tomorrow, reduction of internal social friction will have been accomplished by a much more effective process, one with longer-term possibilities unthinkable under a regime of armed totalitarianism: an education of the individual that prepares him to be satisfied *only* with that society which meets his full range of psychic needs at the same time that it serves the social-developmental needs of its people as a group.

This evolutionary outcome establishes a formula by which theoretical contradictions of post-industrial social life might be resolved in the better interests of humanity. But the education of individuals who are adapted to the complexities of that social life cannot rest on the theme of "man alone." The attempt of man, as the possessor of an advanced technology and culture, to reintegrate himself with nature can ultimately be judged successful or failing only to the degree in which he proves his ability to function once again as an interdependent in a chain of life of which he forms no more than a single link. Ecological balance rests upon the performance of *man* in the world from henceforth, because his power over other life forms now verges upon the absolute. This strongly suggests the impossibility of achieving any relevant education, least of all a general environmental one, without appropriate moral-behavioral content. No human in tomorrow's crowded world can afford, both for his own sake and for that of the race, to elevate himself in either body or spirit at the expense of supportive life in the delicately balanced physical milieu roundabout him.

So then, to sum up, the objectives of a general environmental education will be as reductionist or as broad as teachers and society care to make them, but they will invariably relate to adaptive performances, which in turn are based on individualized criteria. This brings us to the main problem of method in such an education. It is in the nature of a general education, since in an environmental age it must reflect a constantly expanding shape of reality as perceived by the individual, to fall short of its ideal the more it is characterized by a divorce of the data-gathering and abstract learning functions from the opportunity to participate in meaningful learning experiences. This may indicate, but not necessarily, that the days of the physically discrete schoolhouse, with its tiers and rows of yet more discrete schoolrooms, are numbered. The overarching need of today's and tomorrow's learners will continue to be the establishment of optimum conditions under which individuals and groups can test abstract knowledge or pure data against the environment they inhabit. This desideratum cannot be realized simply by the erection of a building with four walls and roof, no matter how much open space is contained therein. It will likely best be obtained by providing a setting in which the components of educational experience are exploited in a general, natural way, as they are encountered in natural environments. The artificial, specialist-dominated school setting with which everyone is familiar and against which today's younger critics have wildly inveighed does not in and of itself guarantee failure. It merely stands in the way, as far as most learners are concerned, of the large-scale shifts in the organization of learning experiences that are implicit in the construct of environmental education.

Fortunately, perhaps, for formal education in its efforts to respond institutionally to socioenvironmental needs, there has now arrived on the scene an innovation which, in theory, goes some distance toward meeting a standard of greater flexibility in formal learning. This is of course the "open school." Open education, with its stronger emphasis on the principles of informality and individualization, has achieved (and will probably for some time to come continue to achieve) its successes mainly on the elementary school level.

In her address "Reflections and Projections Concerning Open Education," Lady Plowden has explained not only what open education is about but also and incidentally what general environmental education has to do with: "What do I mean by open education? I think I mean a learning situation in school where the growth of the personality of the child is more important than the teaching of separate examinable subjects."[17] It follows, in the thinking of this leader in the open education movement, therefore, that "schools must join in society, more actively involving parents, social workers, employers, and administrators as well as educators."[18]

At least in its theoretical framework, this movement appears to offer that kind of broad social basis suited to the educational needs of immediate future generations. But technically, and perhaps in some of its philosophical fuzziness, its application to the reality of contemporary school learning must remain quite limited. The difficulty of application, naturally, increases as one rises through the grade structure. That age span from the early teens through the college undergraduate years typically includes those youth most in need of guidance and effective teaching, for they have reached the *sturm und drang* of adolescence and beginning adulthood and can never again dwell in the more relaxed atmosphere that surrounds the younger child's thought process. And while the teens and youth have reached the stage when detail can be assimilated much more efficiently, they face two problems equally the phenomena of their age status: they require that their learning experiences excite and maintain interest, and they have begun to look searchingly beyond the façade of detail toward the meanings that are revealed only through adult reflection and continuous mental effort. The conditions of learning that are provided for such young people cannot be established without a consideration of these two associated problems. Youth can not achieve success wholly through spongelike efficiency in handling the detail of subject matter *per se*.

It is in the middle or junior high school that youthful

minds are typically exposed to the first really heavy assaults from the subject-matter, specialized curriculum. Although a philosophy of "exploratory experiences" for this age level is usually subscribed to by school administrators, the departmental arrangements for instruction resorted to at this point and the familiar lock-step class schedule, with its ubiquitous "passing" intervals between classes, serve effectively to form (even as they did in Dewey's heyday) a particular understanding by the student of what the educative process is all about: a series of onerous tasks of gleaning from a succession of subject-matter "specialists" myriad separate items of data which, while they may make him better prepared to carry out some specialized task in life (turning one . . . screw or handle on a certain instrument or machine), are destined in the majority of cases to remain everlastingly compartmentalized in the individual's inert mind and (what is more crucial) to fail in any significant way to influence his patterns of behavior; this is the real argument against today's formal education systems and the real argument for a more flexible, more general, and more environmental education.

Tied in closely with this failure of the school is the issue of time lag. For the most part, a youth in seventh or eighth grade has at least another half dozen years to put in at his formal education before more than a very few of the innumerable bits of factual or conceptual data he is expected to acquire can be put to use. To qualify as assimilated knowledge, knowledge in the abstract must be incorporated into some pattern of meaningful experience. Here the formal system tends increasingly to break down, especially after the child reaches junior high school. The experience of learning remains incomplete, among other reasons because basic information or abstractions learned as such cannot be applied at all or are not applied soon enough.

In short, continuity of learning has been defeated by unacceptable delays in reaching a significant stage of application. What is important to the environmental behaviorist in analyzing the implications of this delay is the massive *frustration* it induces in the individual, who must always wait for something to happen, for "real life" to begin. Persons who fancy themselves expert amateur psychologists are apt to parrot expressions like "A little frustration will be a good thing for Johnny. It helps prepare him for the hard knocks of adult life." World trends socially and economically appear to be leading constantly in the direction of increasing the intensity and amount of frustration that all humans must endure. But much laboratory research (notably that of Skinner, with its wide applicability to human learning, especially with regard to the universality of the so-called Law of Effect[19]), as well as the weight of professional opinion generally, seems to support the belief that, beyond a minimum level, the buildup of elements of frustration as an increment of the learning experience must lead to unhappiness and nonadaptation of the organism. Buildup of frustration because of incompleteness of experience appears nowhere more than with the teenager and youth. If school did not loom so large in the existence of these age groups, it might be useless to speak of actions to reduce the burden of frustration by reorganizing the system of formal learning. But school does dominate the life of the young person; and schooling *can* be changed, at least to the extent that vested interests are able to yield some of their pride of position to the prior needs of the learner and of society as a whole.

Nevertheless, one errs signally if he leaps to the easy assumption that subject-matter specialization constitutes a unitary and already well-defined "public enemy." This is an overreaction. Subject matter considered as an unavoidable organization of some related elements of common knowledge lies at the base of anything men have thus far found worthy of investigation or study. One needs to mull over the question: Can man continue to make sense of the infinitely expanding quantities of factual data he is receiving about so many aspects of the universe he inhabits without the organizational framework of subject matter and the system of specialization?

The problem, however, becomes more and more one of placing subject matter and/or specialization in an appropriate context. To determine this context, we must examine alternative philosophies of the school and also alternative administrative arrangements. We must be willing if necessary to reassess the school's position and function in society. This is of course too large an order for this volume, although some discussion of substantive school reorganization will be taken up in the later chapter titled "Nature, Nurture, and the Environmental School of Tomorrow." What does remain to be discussed here is the teacher-student relationship against a backdrop of general environmental educational effort.

The immediate source of our concern must be the relation of a teacher's view of knowledge and the knowledge-transmittal process to a student's power of absorbing knowledge and assimilating it meaningfully rather than mechanically and without meaning. The difference between meaningful and mechanical reception of the substance of a learning experience is central to the problem of general education. Both the teacher's and the student's point of approach to the learning process is complex and difficult of analysis, and the essential qualities of the potentially effective teacher, since these appear to constitute variables of major concern, must be considered in dealing with the teacher-learner interface.

The preparation of a teacher best suited to aid the general educational development of students cannot be separated from the kind of situation in which he is to function. Lacking advance knowledge of the specifics of a situation not to arise until some unknown future date, we are quite unable to lay down precise qualifications to govern his *formal* advance preparation. Facing the nub of this difficulty, state legislative committees on teacher certification and their aides from state departments of education struggle year after year to formulate requirements best suited to insure both a special and a general background in one and the same teacher candidate. With this accomplished on the purely technical level, they typically rest their case. But they have ignored, because at this stage society still expects them to ignore, the real issue in defining generalized capability: what the candidate's *total* preparation and personality amount to. With the steady emergence of environmental behavioral standards and the ever-increasing importance of the general factor in the teaching-learning process, the environmental realist can no longer permit himself this luxury of omission. Indeed, to the environmentalist the kind of teacher needed to educate for adaptation to the general pressures of future life and to the effects of rapid change *can* be described — in terms of background of experience and personal qualities.

As the process of social rationalization invades the teaching profession, a veritable host of factors now operative in judging a job candidate (e.g., specialist background or intentions, accumulation of prior teaching experience on a basis of length of service only, etc.) will diminish in importance compared to his breadth and depth of general experience, formal and informal. Bluntly stated, with an increasing pressure for breadth of competency (rather than pure specialization) as the goal of the formal learning process, decision-makers in education will have no choice other than to seek in their teaching candidates a reflection of this same emphasis. The kind of teacher most needed for an environmental age, in short, will be as much or more a generalist as a specialist. He will have some breadth of knowledge in a good many specialized subject areas, but he has not made the error of over-specializing, so that he has fitted himself to teach only graduate students rather than the far more numerous and (in the mass society) needful junior and senior high and two-year college students. Bound by the excessive state requirements and local social pressures acting to influence teacher candidate selection, school administrators and board will indeed find it difficult to adjust to this essentially liberalizing trend in meeting new demands from society at large for relevance in the teaching process. But at a time when too many time-servers, male and female, are overcrowding the teaching market, and when old concepts such as tenure are being subject to ever more serious public questioning, the trend toward establishing broader criteria of general teaching capability and the paramountcy of an adequately general background of experience as the decisive factors in teacher selection should come into its own.

The existing constrictions of a single salary schedule and the union attitude toward the quality-of-performance issue (in which a worker's effectiveness as a member of his profession's pressure group means everything and his effectiveness in teaching means little or nothing) must under these newly changed circumstances recede decisively from view. Salaries will be negotiated individually, under a different set of assumptions regarding how individual effectiveness in teaching may be judged, one in which a computer-monitored contract for teacher performance, a contract covering many phases of the teaching process now ignored as intangible and immeasurable, will play an important role. The elaboration of such a scheme cannot be attempted here, but a few of its basic implications for the future public concept of the "new" teacher should be sketched out.

The socioeconomic pressures of a world order subject to constantly broadened rationalization of all goal-attainment techniques and practices have invaded the domain of formal education, with the result that many shibboleths of an earlier time are under serious question, for example, "more is better"; "he knows his subject, therefore he is as good a teacher as we could ever find." Administrators whose lip-service has been given to "absolute top quality in all our teachers" and who in practice are only too satisfied with teachers against whom few or no complaints are made — these men and women in positions of authority will find their decisions subject to increasing public criticism, because they are decisions made in the sole interest of administrative convenience and largely ignore long-term learner needs. Much of this mounting problem has to do with the unwise restraints placed by legal, administrative, and social requirements upon the selection of the best teachers in the general sense, teachers who are known to have

much to offer younger learners since the teachers themselves
have not stopped learning.

To the skilled, adaptive teacher of this kind, the subject
field he may be nominally responsible for is only a point of
beginning, not an end in itself. To this person other skills,
such as empathy, concern, understanding, accessibility,
are far too important to leave to chance; he works constantly
at their development in himself, and also at the development
of these capabilities *par excellence* in educational science
itself, as a *method* of achieving optimum communication in
the learning interchange. Out of all this, and transcending it,
he also presents a model of behavior with which youth not
only can, but *must*, identify.

This educator is perhaps no paragon of detailed knowledge,
but he is a superior adaptive, and on this basis he qualifies
particularly as a model for his students. He is not only open
to change; he also acts as a *bona fide* agent of change. Newness to him is not, as it has become to so many teachers,
something to be resisted as unnecessary and personally
dangerous. He accepts new data or new hypotheses in science
or new developments in the arts as accruals to public knowledge and therefore of private interest, regardless of his
subjective reaction to them. He encourages youth to maintain
and develop an open attitude to change, seeing each newly
arriving package of unanticipated stimuli as something to be
studied carefully and adequately pondered rather than
summarily rejected. He shows by his own willingness to go
"one more mile" in seeking the answer to some disturbing
problem that he expects the same performance from them.

This teacher is not academic, in the typical narrow sense.
He has done more than merely to go through college and
teacher training and straight into classroom teaching. His
credit hours in some major field of academic concentration,
upon which the public school administrative mind fastens
with its peculiar form of "tunnel vision," *must* rate far down
the line in his list of priorities. (Indeed, the tendency of the
"normal" administrative mentality to confuse willingness to

promote change with a threat to the system of control, or an individual's moral and mental independence with positive insubordination, remains possibly the single most serious barrier to the emergence of the "new" teacher of whom I am speaking.)

So then, this newer, more nearly ideal teacher has as much a nonprofessional as a strictly professional background of experience that he brings to the formal learning situation. Typically, he has worked at a variety of jobs outside academia, has traveled, and has reflected on life's problems far more than he has unthinkingly waded into them as an unruly activist. He has acquired a conspicuous breadth of outlook inconsistent with the ruling provincialism of the old localist education; he has also evolved a sense of his mission in life, a sense of social and individual values suitable to an age of rapid change, and a sense of his own ability to contribute positively to the direction of such change. He does not waste effort in wildly fighting the remains of yesterday's power structure. He tolerates but at no time accepts blindly such old-era rigidities as the teacher certification system, with its systematic imposition of a narrow administrative outlook upon what is essentially a free mental process, namely learning. He does not "fight city hall" with futile direct actions, for he prefers steady pressure in the direction of substantive change, however modest and piecemeal, to the radical push for instant and total change, with its tendency to induce violent resistance, backlash, and continuance of pressures and counterpressures, which in the final analysis are likely to promote narrow or anti-democratic interests.

Until this individual is represented in every classroom, there will be precious little *general* learning in formal education. And without general learning, there can be little successful individualization, unless by the latter we mean keeping each student (like some animal on a stock farm) fed up to his capacity with the minute items of endless data that form merely the subject-matter ground for a specialized education and may have no relation of any significance to the adaptive, general environmental education here under discussion. Such individualization can only be meaningless in an environmental context, since it leaves stultified the learner's ability to link abstract knowledge and concrete experience. If this is the extent of general learning, then significant progress toward the essential end of environmental integration has hardly even begun.

A Necessary Conclusion

We should remind ourselves of what remains implicit in what has been said in this and in earlier chapters, that as long as overt behavior plays so potentially dislocating a role in social life, an education that does not incorporate as a principal aim the shaping of mass human behavior more and more carefully to environmental purposes is insufficient. Because environmental limitations affect human life development in a variety of ways (theoretically approaching the absolute), a general education for the coming age must first and foremost succeed in freeing the individual in advance of those urges leading to psychologically inappropriate behavior. Nothing so much suggests the balance-point between man and milieu needed for environmental adaptation as the ideal of judgment suggested in Shakespeare's phrase *Ripeness is all.* But I am speaking in the main of young people, who must learn in a relatively short time and through experiences few in number how to respond to life in a complex society, a life that for the individual can be made difficult to the point of intolerability by his own behavioral errors.

Specialized and subject-matter training cannot, in spite of frequent spin-off effects on pupils of developing enthusiasm, interest, absorption in the minutiae of a field of study, and so forth, adequately insure cultivation of favorable patterns of general behavior. It seems clear that to a considerable extent the individual, especially in the advanced democratic societies, is in a position from an early age to follow all too freely his own short-term predispositions for one or another line of behavior; he teaches himself, in other words, and is relatively immune to the efforts of others who would *consciously* seek to influence him to move counter to his own predilictions. In these societies, given the danger posed by the buildup of trends toward mass antisocial behavior over recent generations, planning to secure those changes in the individual's affective environment which will prevent him from learning an excess of unfavorable behavior patterns is both desirable and unavoidable. Yet, while planning obviously implies establishment of powerful systems of educational stimuli acting to enhance adaptive behavior, at the same time those who design and apply such systems must be constantly on guard to see that in the course of their activity the inner core of each learner's individuality is maintained in accordance with the democratic concept of intellectual freedom.

Any attempt to assert that open schools will solve such complex problems as these unaided would amount to ludicrous presumption. The same appears to hold true for other prescriptions for obtaining massive improvements by applying formula remedies. Thus the concept of behavioral objectives, when viewed in the light of environmental realities, may well provide significant new input to educational theory *if* the concept can be reconciled with a more global philosophy of environmental education. This would, of course, require the introduction of value considerations (e.g., the relative superiority for purposes of adaptation of one kind of learning experience to another), anathema to the present generation of behavioral objectivists. In any case, behavior narrowly prescribed by those who view a human response to be elicited as acontextual or defined as one would define the performance of a rat working through a maze or a pigeon developing on-cue behavior to obtain a pellet of food — such behavior cannot in the present incomplete knowledge of learning and behavioral processes be shown to relate other than peripherally to an attack on the complexities involved in any comprehensive study of contemporary *human* learning and behavior.

Teachers who are in the main academically oriented specialists will ordinarily have too narrow a range of behavior and perception of others to create those conditions of learning which promote in students environmentally adaptive capabilities. On the plane of psychological functioning solely, I would say that such teachers do fail to develop effective learning among their students, or for that matter fail to develop suitable motivation to learn at all in any environmental sense. This may not be entirely their fault, since the prescriptive and traditional character of formal schooling allows them so little leeway for experimentation. But it is doubtful that even under more open conditions these teachers could do their jobs in the way required under tomorrow's stern pressures. For by tomorrow's standards they will fail on the two counts that, as Gilbert Highet made clear, separate the teacher from other professional men and from businessmen and workers: they cannot create a bridge between school or college and the real world for the student; they cannot create that other bridge so needed by the student, between his present youth and the maturity toward which his every action leads.[20] The general environmental adaptations for which the student must have intense and effective guidance are foreign to the average and below-average teacher of today because such teachers have not made, nor ever will make, their own adaptations at this higher, more demanding level of response.[21] Even free from the crushing weight of an overly formal operating structure of teaching (a structure, indeed that may in itself provide the only organizational and psychological motivation that most second-rate pedagogues ever experience), these men and women would lack the independence of standard social expectations by which they could provide young people with exemplary models of leadership behavior — necessary as never before, given the extraordinary moral confusion and intellectual uncertainty faced by contemporary youth as it struggles to sort out its imperatives for today and tomorrow.

What are needed are probably not more but *fewer* teachers.

This terrifying suggestion of course flies directly in the face of the conventional wisdom of schoolmen, unionists, teacher preparers, and all other educational professionals with a vested interest in resistance to change. But quality, in the end, must assert itself over merely quantitative considerations, because it represents the operative environmental principle in action. We should not forget that quality is the general, all-embracing phenomenon, the one we must resort to when quantitative factors cancel each other out and we are still left with the need to compare one organism or one experience — or one education — with another. It alone supplies the missing, intangible element that a too-specialized organism or experience — or education — lacks for wholeness or symmetry or ultimate viability in a world with, after all, limited tolerance for anything specialized to the point of meaninglessness. It fits with the new vision of a man suited to life in the environmental age: one who can direct human learning and behavior, his own and others', with maximum effect and minimum friction, in the interest of a constantly more balanced life in the natural universe.

5
The Traditional Learning and Development of Environmental Behavior

We have always and persistently striven in our formal under-taking of education to make students ever more aware of fields of *definable* knowledge. Behind this principle of op-eration lies an assumption: that the student possesses an ability to put such knowledge to intelligent use. This may prove, in today's hard-fact world — to say nothing of tomorrow's — a wrong assumption. An erosion of this single-minded view of what the learning-behavior process is all about seems now to be underway and appears indeed to be speeding up as thoughtful people recognize how much the pace of change in cybernated societies has quickened. Yet schools remain by and large wedded to the old view, that if one makes a positive frontal attack on the body of developed knowledge, he is provided with a suitable education. Should it be wondered at that critics ask scathingly whether or not schools will ever turn out a decent product if they continue in their present state of organization?

115

Behind the façade of formalism that characterizes every classroom situation there exists a second-order set of phenomena. These are peoples' emotional states, conditions of mind accompanying the surface conformity to rational tasks and objective behavior. One may err in opposite directions in considering the effect of these "matching" phenomena on learning: by assuming their lack of significance or by assuming their over-significance. The extent to which emotions theoretically govern learning on any *specific* occasion hardly concerns the environmental thinker. His problem, rather, is what the compound of emotions and cognitions makes of an individual's behavior over time. To him the strength of any socially integrated individual living in a complex industrial society will be measured in terms of the use of emotions to forward genuine growth of the person and genuine social purposes. This positive adaptation is consistently a major issue to anyone concerned seriously for human values in an age of social stress and readjustment to new realities.

Before the motif of environment surfaced, there was lacking any valid reference point around which a common focus upon so complicated a web of relationships could be developed. This does not imply, of course, that overnight environmentalism can become a millennial talisman by which mankind may be led surely and safely out of the wilderness of complication that modern life entails. At this stage environmentalism does not define with precision limitations on individual rights or ambitions. Too minutely formulated, it could become a new scourge, a *lex talionis* more medieval in intent than modern, no matter how sophisticated the technology that supports it. But in a world that has seen the rapid and often largely unnoticed drift into cybernation, and that has witnessed an imposition of varied and subtle systems of control upon both individuals and groups, subliminally more than overtly, without the aware consent of those affected — in such a world manipulation of the human psyche tends to occur routinely, its intent being frankly to bring about predictable outcomes of behavior. The academic community has not to this point absorbed the significance for itself of this rationalization of the emotional resources of a mass society.

Nevertheless, one cannot help wondering at the needs of that society, needs that might better be filled by reordering and redirecting the services of the formal education network. Inveighing against irrationalism and the manipulation of emotions toward narrow goals is a natural academic reaction under present circumstances, but not a sufficient one. In a world of unlimited physical resources perfectly utilized and controlled by technology, and assuming an unlimited capacity on the part of the human species to adapt to struggle and resist defeat, then indeed no meaning could attach to the concept of learning for survival behavior. But we do not inhabit such a utopia; the coming environmental age will be characterized by Malthusian imperatives to which adaptation must be made — and probably under conditions of greater stress and uncertainty than were ever before, in the slower-moving past, known to man.

With regard to the traditional learning and its typical modes of transmission, then, a serious question can be posed: Should the commitment to objectivism and rationalism inherited from the Enlightenment and dominant in all formal education since that time continue so to dominate in a newer era, that of environmental learning? Does this tradition suit the new learner? In short, are there sufficient reasons to permit this unitary approach to have exclusive sway in contemporary learning when the latter involves not so much answers as questions and must be intended to equip individuals with no power so much as that over themselves?

The Young Child

Anyone who has watched young children, or even at times older ones, in a learning situation must be struck by their constantly shifting level of emotional involvement. This show of positive (or negative) interest in all its varied manifestations clearly underlies the whole learning process. Dewey expressly referred to this dynamic quality of the child's interaction with experience when he stated: "If the living, experiencing being is an intimate participant in the activities of the world to which it belongs, then knowledge is a mode of participation, valuable to the degree in which it is effective."[1]

Dewey's comment seems to speak against the concept of educational experience as "better" the more devoid of affective/participatory content it can be made. But pursuit of cognitive knowledge structured in a straight-line fashion through time, without extensive regard for the element of subjective and immediately social concerns, manifestly remains the chief stock in trade of formal schools. Despite efforts to "individualize" teaching materials and to widen the use of such practices as the inquiry technique, this remains also the major point of attack for the "software" industries, to which the formal system of schooling is allied and which would stand to suffer severe financial setbacks if individual schools became self-sufficient in learning ideas and materials.

One significant result of this lag in educational practice has been an inadequate development of the individual's ability to respond effectively and critically to stimuli designed to channel his behavior by controlling in some degree his affective states. One errs if he sees this problem as historical or cultural or pedagogical only. It is all of these, and an axiological problem as well. It exists wherever and whenever the "whole" individual has been left merely half formed, or shaped into the behavioral mechanism for realization of someone else's ambition.

• Simpler moral tyrannies of earlier times, like those of Savonarola or Cromwell, of course gave way in modern times to far more fully exploitative, well-organized efforts (e.g., Communism, Naziism) to create a malleable society, propagandized continually to insure maximum mass conformity. By destroying the individual's right to self-development, all such movements educate to perversity. But they differ in method, not in intent, only marginally from the great cybernated, manipulative institutions of today's free capitalistic societies, institutions that also educate, spearheaded by the vanguard of Madison Avenue's idea men, to perverse actions whose foundation is invariably a standardized emotion cultivated with much care to the exclusion of competing emotions, or thought for personal consequences.

The point is that it would be altogether reasonable to postulate, given conditions of contemporary life in industrial societies, that mass behavior directed at a subliminal level may not be capable of redirection simply by exposing the individual to a system of purely cognitive educative experiences. Nor will the addition of a few adjunct experiences of sensitivity training, or even the psychiatrist's ministrations, bring the desired effects to more than a minuscule number of people. Only education (or, perhaps better reeducation) of masses of individuals at the level of popular reaction, of instinctive behavior, would seem able to permit such redirection of mass behavior. And this means an education of the right kind provided at the right time in the individual's life cycle.

Piaget's work with young children's learning patterns is important for a variety of reasons, especially for his careful delineation of the child's growth through several maturational stages. For the theorist of environmental behavior as for the developmental psychologist, these steps in the developmental process do more than suggest guidelines for the organization of learning experiences. They are significant as much for what they reveal of the child's ability at various stages *not* to perform certain cognitive functions and moral judgments as to perform them. This point is of great importance in environmental learning because it implies a theoretical optimum sequence of learning experiences once goals of the educative process have been set.

Piaget's cognitive theory, which has been, generally speaking, the most influential and pragmatically based system of interpretation of children's learning in contemporary times,[2] holds that in normal circumstances a subject cannot achieve essential cognitive competence until there has been attained a corresponding state of physical and mental maturation. Understanding is a process of subsuming data from the world around and explaining the data in a manner that the state of development of the mind at that moment permits. For the theoretician of environmental learning, it becomes a matter of significance to investigate ways and means of maximizing the special opportunities for adaptive learning that are inherent in each of these developmental steps, with their built-in limitations of perception and reasoning.

This issue is too complex to be dealt with here in any detail. It would seem appropriate, however, to consider one pertinent feature of Piaget's system that has particular applicability to this question. This is the counterproof, an element of the Piaget interview procedure that more than any other tends to bring the child face to face with mental frustration and may reveal twists of mind or intellectual habits indicative of ways of meeting future problems he may encounter.

Counterproof is in fact a prototype of the mental flex- ibility that the better-adapted individual must develop and redevelop through an entire lifetime in order to function in a complex society. It is a means, in short, for young or old, of combating the premature mental closure that frustration in goal-attainment visits upon anyone in such a society at regular intervals, particularly in respect to tasks that require the marshaling of considerable intellectual resources. Piaget's use of this device as a formal component of his interview procedure specifies its use, typically, by an adult interviewer interacting with a single subject, a child of elementary or junior high school age. The learning stimuli may be of various kinds: building blocks, a balance scale with weights of several sizes, perhaps a set of marbles, or containers of different shapes to be filled with sand or pellets, and so on. These stimuli, at the interviewer's direction, will be experimented with physically by the child.

Depending on the child's level of cognitive development,

his explanation of the phenomena he has experienced will tend to reveal his ability to use conceptual understanding (e.g., the principle of reversibility) in accounting for observed events. There will be fairly standard reactions to these learning situations in each of Piaget's major developmental stages (i.e., sensory-motor; preoperational; concrete operational; formal operational). Inability to account for a particular observed event in terms of adult logic is routinely expected, the subtlety and relative accuracy of the explanation varying with the child's developmental status. After the child has presented his own explanation of cause and effect, the interviewer is ready to employ the technique of counterproof.

Counterproof consists essentially of the interviewer's opening up the possibilities for alternative solutions to the problem at hand. Without pointing out the obvious falsity of the child's findings, the interviewer asks if the subject might not give some consideration to other cause-effect explanations than that initially hit upon.

What this procedure implies with regard to teaching is the importance of helping children to consider how they come by their ideas. That is to say, one thing Piaget emphasizes as a goal of education is to get children to check their ideas and not to accept as valid the first thought that comes to mind. Presenting alternative ideas, as in the contr' épreuve, is a way of getting children to check their ideas without the onus of right or wrong, particularly when the alternative idea is presented tentatively.[3]

This approach is environmentally important, for one thing, because it goes beyond the didactic, explanatory approach. But, even beyond this, it has the broad, humbling influence of introducing the neophyte to the specter of the unknown in questions of causation. Any mind too satisfied with easy first explanations of physical causality, of number, and the like, fails to develop a critical sense. One can readily appreciate this feature's importance in any scheme of environmental learning.

Essential to Piaget's system, too, is the understanding

that explanations that the child can develop to give a more suitable version of what he has just experienced will still correspond intellectually to his level of development. At each of these stages of mental growth, Piaget's theory seems to imply (and his evidence as recorded in numerous publications amply substantiates) that it would be theoretically possible to design optimum learning experiences in which the child is exposed to those critical issues bearing on the interrelatedness of physical and mathematical phenomena. The subject would not be expected to perform at a level exceeding his capabilities at the time, but he would have to exercise vigorous use of his powers of thought to range over and evaluate a series of alternative interpretations suited to his capacities and developmental status. In the environmental framework this becomes significant not because of the amount of pure knowledge the individual can accumulate at each stage of the growth process but because of the habits of mind it elicits.

Today's school organization, with its emphasis on *classroom* activities as the primary basis of individual learning, often does not permit individual students to maintain a steady development through these stages. Partly, as the contrast between the interview learning setting and the typical classroom setting would imply, the child cannot with the amount of help he is given in the classroom follow enough of the general thread of experience in the way that would permit him to optimize his pattern of intellectual growth; partly, too, he is the victim of innumerable distractions arising through the social nature of the classroom, and partly he simply suffers from a great deal of what would probably be poor teaching, whether presented to a single child in a private room or to a classroom of thirty-five or forty.

And yet, in spite of such problems, children do learn. Test results, year after year, tend to exhibit a kind of mass progress among the population of school children at large, which suggests that formalistic, academic, objectivist, classroom education does produce in the overall some measurable change, however slight, for the better. But while this may be the case, and it surely ought to be admitted in the interests of realistic thinking, we are nevertheless left dissatisfied when we apply the criterion of environmental adaptation to this traditional learning. Today more people (as a percentage of the population) may put their learning to use and log more moments of mental search and reconsideration of impulse behavior than at any time in history. But the question remains, Has this improved education really produced learning that allows human beings to pursue environmental adaptation more successfully, or has their learning only served to lead them up more blind alleys and make them prey to more nonadaptive behavior?

This question leads us to reexamine the traditional learning, looking for a gap in it that might explain why the question would be answered negatively by so many to whom it might be put. With its objectivist bias, the traditional learning has tended to leave to one side any possibility of imposing values upon the learner, except as these are generated spontaneously in the course of regular activities in the academic sequence of learning. In this matter the directed pursuit of traditional learning is allied with the traditional ethos of Western democracy, which holds that the individual is supreme in determining the values he will espouse. For practical purposes, this manner of proceeding, however appropriate from the ethical standpoint, places serious pressures upon both learner and teacher in contemporary formal education. To the extent that there does exist a break between intention and outcome in traditional education, it appears to center on this point: that the moral side of education is left to chance and that where it does come into the picture it is in no systematic way coordinated with academic learning. In a system permitting total sway of the individualistic pursuit of self-interest, this gap would hardly matter; in a system of education ever more constrained to mold the individual to environmental imperatives, it becomes a source of constantly growing difficulty.

The literature of educational philosophy is replete with

124   ENVIRONMENT AND LEARNING

expressions of the need for inculcation of moral principles in the child. Plato, Quintillian, Comenius, Rousseau, and Pestalozzi are a few of the standard writers who have developed this subject. At many points in the classic writings (especially in Froebel), the importance of early experiences in which the moral sense is tested and reinforced is stressed. But only a residuum of practical usefulness comes down to us from these earlier thinkers as we seek to develop ways and means of educating for moral behavior in this, our contemporary world. We find it necessary to fall back on more contemporary thought and a more analytic approach to the problem.

It is not perhaps surprising that very early in his long career of child study Piaget became concerned about the development of moral values. His work in this area is worth reviewing in the present context. Piaget's observations led him to posit a series of developmental stages through which the child passes in his moral, as in his intellectual, development. From the infantile stage of pure self-centeredness, the infant tends gradually to become aware of differences between himself and elements of the surrounding world.

> Just as at first the mind, before it can dissociate what belongs to objective laws from what is bound up with the sum of subjective conditions, confuses itself with the universe, so does the individual begin by understanding and feeling everything through the medium of himself before distinguishing what belongs to things and other people from what is the result of his own particular intellectual and affective perspective. At this stage, therefore, the individual cannot be conscious of his own thought, since consciousness of self implies a perpetual comparison of the self with other people.[4]

Little by little the sense of differential norms of behavior grows, roughly paralleling the child's intellectual development. There is a "kinship between logical and ethical norms. Logic is the morality of thought just as morality is the logic of action."[5] In not too long a time more, through observation and experience of adult control in his life, the child acquires certain moral perspectives that come increasingly to govern his behavior.

> Just as the child believes in the adult's omniscience so also does he unquestioningly believe in the absolute value of the imperatives he receives. The result of this unilateral respect is of great practical value, for it is in this way that there is formed an elementary sense of duty and the first normative control of which the child is capable. But . . . this acquisition [is] sufficient to form true morality. For conduct to be characterized as moral there must be something more than an outward agreement between its content and that of the commonly accepted rules: it is also requisite that the mind should tend towards morality as to an autonomous good and should itself be capable of appreciating the value of the rules that are proposed to it.[6]

This stage involves an exaggeration, due to inexperience, of the reasons for obedient behavior. After a time the child passes to a higher state of understanding. Then,

> by comparing his own private motives with the rules adoped by each and sundry, the individual is led to judge objectively the acts and commands of other people, including adults. Whence the decline of unilateral respect and the primacy of personal judgment. But in consequence of this, cooperation suppresses both egocentrism and moral realism, and thus achieves interiorization of rules. A new morality follows upon that of pure duty . . . . Obedience withdraws in favour of the idea of justice and of mutual service, now the source of all the obligations which till then had been imposed as incomprehensible commands. In a word, cooperation on the moral plane brings about transformations exactly parallel to those . . . in the intellectual domain.[7]

Piaget does not view the individual's moral progress through childhood as any less significant to society than his intellectual progress. There is some importance that attaches, therefore, to a learning program that can develop more than minimum individual adherence to sociomoral imperatives.

> The adult must be a collaborator and not a master, from this double point of view, moral and rational. But conversely, it would be

unwise to rely upon biological 'nature' alone to ensure the dual progress of conscience and intelligence, when we realize to what extent all moral as all logical norms are the result of cooperation. Let us therefore try to create in the school a place where individual experimentation and reflection carried out in common come to each other's aid and balance one another.[8]

The work of Piaget is not considered at such length in this context merely because it forms the single most credible and widely discussed body of developmental learning theory currently extant. Rather, these essential points from that theory are presented because they confirm the dual (i.e., intellectual *and* moral) nature of the growth process and they suggest a range of possibilities for need change in the formal education of the mass of young children. Even a brief comparison of the experience of counterproof by way of a Piaget-type of interview and the usual classroom exposition of a similar learning experience seems to give empirical evidence of how, increasingly, traditional modes of instruction fail to provide an educaton for realistic adaptation. This would appear to hold true for the moral, as well as the intellectual, domains of learning, and since both moral and intellectual growth are necessities for adaptive behavior now and in the future, traditional forms of education are evidently becoming less and less relevant to the child's adaptive needs.

Open-space schools, the nongraded system, and other experimental efforts to vary elementary-level schooling have served to focus attention on the mechanics of change. They have not served as well to clarify *directions* for change, and from an environmental standpoint we are left to a considerable degree where we began. In some part this situation arises out of the fact that these new "ways of doing" are merely alterations in a mode of teaching and learning; they still direct the learner entirely toward the old *goals* of education, which are the accumulation of factual knowledge for its own sake and the preservation of a standard of false objectivity in adaptation.

The child's energies are mainly applied to apprehending

and interpreting his immediate environment; this factor of behavior can be assumed regardless of cultural circumstances. Only children in the categories of the gifted or the mentally retarded are possible exceptions. This places a severe burden on the school. If the normal, average child is to evolve away from acts that are cumulatively nonadaptive and toward patterns of more adaptive behavior, he needs appropriate stimulation in the direction of the latter. His early education must involve those experiences which use his powers of apprehension and interpretation to set him farther along the path of adaptation. When we experiment in the schools without a goal in view such as producing an environmentally adapted individual, we are introducing open spaces or nongradedness for our own purposes and not the learner's; we are introducing change only to promote change.

As we evaluate the end product of an elementary school education, the child who in North America is promoted out of fifth or sixth grade and into middle or junior high school, we are often aware that this individual's understanding of physical causality or of moral necessity may be quite underdeveloped. We observe that his behavior does not conform to expectation. We have been looking for indications that he can and will react in line with norms of behavior at least suitable to his developmental status. We seek evidence that he has become sensitive to the problems of cause-effect reasoning and the problems of others in society. Even at this early stage of the child's development, we find ourselves disappointed in him.

In seeking to explain this disappointment, we talk of how the dynamic contradictions of modern society have even invaded the school itself: the trend toward greater allowance for idiosyncratic individual behavior as against the increasing rationalization of social and economic group life; the toleration of divergent life styles as against the growing insistence on conformity within organizational structures. Yet a shadow hangs over all our efforts at explanation. As adults, we are too knowledgeable about the behavioral necessities of a contemporary industrial society. We are too aware of what the child will face as he emerges into adult life later on, that what he should be learning now has escaped him both as a lone individual and as a social being.

Allow the child to live and learn *as a child*. That was Rousseau's philosophy. We in the late twentieth century are loath to overthrow this belief; we shy away from the desentimentalization of childhood, feeling it to be one last aspect of our humanity that we cannot do without. But we know too that today's pleasure does not guarantee tomorrow's security. Society is entering the period of environmental ordering of both human behavior and human intellectual functioning on a mass scale. Impulse control, tolerance for frustration and ambiguity, openness to a variety of intellectual interests, a consistent effort to maintain oneself morally and emotionally (even in the midst of moral and emotional confusion) — although these goals were never actually programmed for the child in the more easygoing days of yesteryear, he was fairly likely to acquire them, given the relative stability of a slowly developing society and the relative social adequacy of the school of that era. Today these qualities constitute the very psychological essence of a successfully adaptive individual and there is a widespread feeling at all levels of society that their cultivation simply does not any longer occur automatically, least of all through formal education.

Can we afford, in short, to emphasize the form of a traditional learning while ignoring its substance in our system of schooling? The forces of rationalization at work in society today bear in on the traditional school with increasing pressure. We are not maintaining this school as a viable social agency, since in its present state of organization it does not develop in the individual, to the degree required, the qualities needed for adaptation. It fails the individual in both intellectual and moral domains of personal development. If this is happening today, then how much worse must be the situation tomorrow, when environmental imperatives

demand even more of the individual and of the social institutions that prepare him for the business of living? Clearly,
the traditional learning and the school as a social organization
are in need of restructuring in line with a newly defined
necessity. For the sake of today's children, who will become
tomorrow's adults, should these challenges not be acknowledged and consciously grappled with?

Later Youth and Traditional Learning: The Onset of Change

It is often remarked by educators that what substantive
change has taken place in formal education has occurred at
the elementary level and that effecting change of any kind
becomes progressively more difficult as one moves up the
ladder of formal schooling. There is an element of folk
wisdom in this observation. Certainly experimentation has
been more widespread at the K-6 level, especially in richer
districts and suburban schools. Too, the more open stance
toward learning of the young child who has not yet acquired
any false patina of social sophistication tends to aid in the
effective transmission of knowledge. It might even be said
that, from the environmental point of view, the typical
elementary school is not at all seriously unsuited to most
children's adaptive needs.

This is not to imply, of course, that K-6 education does
not require a basic redefinition of its goals in light of the
environmental character of future group life. Nor does it
imply that a majority of teachers in elementary schools are
well chosen or well trained, or that taken as a group they
perform at a high enough standard. Here, too, the retrogressive effects of tradition and administrative convenience often
act to obscure basic goals and to make a mockery of the
principle of honest competition in the teaching profession.

Yet by comparison with the schooling of adolescents,
that of younger children represents in the environmental
sense an area of no less significance but far less immediately

pressing need. Partly this is true because of the nature of
adolescence itself, partly because of a growing mismatch
between the student's sociopsychic learning needs and an
excessively artificial curriculum, a curriculum maintained
primarily for reasons which have little to do with the student's needs. Although this curriculum, as the heart of traditional learning, has been so often criticized from so many
different points of view, some comments here regarding its
unsuitability from the basically environmental point of
view are in order.

The core of the difficulty is psychological. Today's adolescent curriculum reflects not today's needs, or much less
tomorrow's, but yesterday's educational prejudices, conceits,
and inflexibilities of an administrative character. It does not
take into account the extent to which contemporary youth
(for all the adult society's self-reassurances that "young
people are the same today as yesterday") *must* learn and
behave differently from school youth of 1910 or 1930.
Today, communication breakthroughs have literally sur-
feited youth with forceful yet psychologically undigestible
stimuli from nonschool sources. These have had the effect
of making young people prematurely aware in a general
sense of the magnitude of their own and of the human
predicament. Our young people are also affectively much
more habituated to seek and accept stimulation, while at the
same time they cannot react effectively to stimuli because
they have not accumulated enough experience to give full
meaning to their behavior.

High schools and colleges in their increasingly standardized functions within society, in their roles as selection agencies for the adult work force, have lost sight of the essence of
education as an emotionally satisfying experience in social
participation. By locking youth into an academic, non-
involving, emotionally sterile, and often actually boring
program of study, schools have held students at a distance
from what is of most significance to the probing, selective
adolescent psyche: the opportunity to identify the self

with emotionally fulfilling, socially credible occupations — occupations that permit, or indeed, compel, individual development of the most diverse and concentrated interests.

Much of this has, of course, been said before in other contexts. It can easily be overstated and be made into little more than another repetitive, unlistened-to complaint. In the environmental context, however, its importance becomes considerably clearer: fullness of experience in learning occupies and satisfies the psyche in its strenuous efforts to accommodate, as youth must always accommodate, to the first massive pressures of adult life. Growth in skillful adaptation can begin in an adult sense at this point or it can be permanently discouraged. To learn behavior that promotes adaptation during this crucial formative period is to acquire learning that cannot help constituting environmental growth. But such learning requires a suitable curriculum, and this means a reexamination of the one we have — the curriculum of traditional learning.

It is an easy matter to say that only a new curriculum, one reflecting current and future needs, meets our requirements. But how does one proceed to bring this "new" curriculum into being? We cannot have it without making substantive change; we will not produce it merely by tacking "something different" as an appendage onto the body of our old curriculum. Conversely, we cannot simply substitute another monolithic structure for the one we now have and still expect success. The variety of forces at work upon young minds, nevertheless, suggests a variety of approaches to curriculum change.

We must begin to take inventory of the different teaching styles, enable teachers that desire to work in a certain style to develop a structure to facilitate their approach, and then carefully describe the different learning options for parents and students so they can make intelligent decisions about their school experience. This would help to move education from a chance to a choice level, and enable parents and students to select educational approaches most conducive to their interests, needs, and learning styles. *I want us*

> *to begin to legitimize the alternative learning experiences so that*
> *parents can at least have two learning environments to choose*
> *between.* [9]

In short, not only variety of approach but also a careful systematization of the processes of teaching and learning must be developed to bring relevance to the school experience. This will involve recognition of the difference between the kind of systematizaton of knowledge that teachers of the traditional learning profess and the kind of systematization of incoming data that appeals naturally to the juvenile mind. This recognition cannot constitute an argument *per se* against learning that is highly discrete and isolated from a meaningful context (e.g., that "fact" which a student cannot place in any ready frame of reference but which he must recall in order to answer an examination question). Rather, it argues against establishing a permanent and obvious didacticism, which uses only the content of traditional learning, as the sole format of all formal learning. Obsession with personnel processing as an end in itself and an evident unwillingness to move toward a system of diversified learning experiences mark the functional props of a retrogressive contemporary school, but any move away from these universally condemned conditions of operation presumes a more attractive alternative. How can such an alternative be defined?

Diversification of curricular opportunities cannot provide the sole answer, of course, any more than a falsely imposed freedom of choice among a number of options, all of which are equally lacking in significance to the chooser. Total individualization of curriculum is the theoretical goal, and in an environmental sense the path to this goal has no *a priori* elements except a common core of socializing and humanizing experiences. Options selected by a parent or by the student himself may well provide a valid indication of learning momentum; life is a continuum through time of innumerable choices, and free choice of what one will do in learning assumes a higher level of motivation to perfect subsequent behavior than if no choice had existed in the learning phase. However, in an age of such great social complexity, individuals, especially those without experience, can hardly be expected to choose wisely a present course of action that will correspond neatly to future needs. Learning for flexibility is therefore of far more importance to the potentially adaptive individual than learning for immediate self-satisfaction.

This, then, constitutes one very large flaw in the "schools of choice" context and creates a firm point of separation between environmental education and education by choice. Another flaw that can be seen in the latter theory is the lack of an immediate and tangible point of reference in a cohesive, self-organizing social group, a group to which the individual can meaningfully attach himself. Against the backdrop of a complex learning process embedded in an even more complex social process, the mere idea of total freedom of choice can hardly be significant in and of itself. It does not become so, does not assume a practical shape, unless it can be merged with some group activity that also conveys intrinsic meaning to the individual.

With adolescents the youthful urge to participate, to *belong*, outweighs, or at the least encompasses as a larger priority, such limited behavioral tasks as memorizing rules or laws of codified knowledge, applying these to wholly theoretical problems, or carrying out individual performances that overstress achievement as a competitive necessity and ignore it as a personal imperative. (The last becomes particularly relevant when we consider the more cohesive social fabric, the climate of greater social control, that future applied environmentalism dictates.) Interaction between youth and a complex environment, if it is to relate to emotional states of learners in a manner consistent with need, must be systematized at a higher functional level, one more nearly matching the activities engaged in to individual perceptions of meaning. Until this closer match is realized in some degree, our standard tradition of learning must be held accountable (along with the professional educators

who resist change in *any* form) for the culturally based
adolescent revolt against formal learning.

The Use and Abuse of Tradition

A tradition loses its human and social significance as it
congeals into culturally repetitive performances and responses. It loses, in a word, it relevance to society. This is the case
now with our tradition of learning as society emerges into a
newer age, one phasing into an environmental era. The growing resistance to this tradition becomes the cutting edge in a
gathering process of social change.

The academic tradition in secondary education has been
built upon two fundamental assumptions about the late
industrial socioeconomic order: a) of an ever-increasing
need in all job markets for persons with precise, specialized
knowledge, with college entrance requirements and the later
college degree constituting merely the next steps in a uni-
form, predetermined career progress for which secondary
education serves as an unquestioned base; b) of the *automatic*
effectiveness of a preordered body of such specialized knowledge, not only in relation to later employment but also in
maintaining learning motivation during the period of formal
education itself. As society evolves and changes, these fixed
assumptions must be reassessed, and their valuable elements
weighed against their disadvantages.

The academic tradition deals with important knowledge,
knowledge (insofar as we can tell in our current state of
partial ignorance) better organized and more pertinent to
what we now see as future requirements than any other.
The directions taken by post-industrial society in its continuing evolution make preservation and enlargement of this
knowledge a first priority. In these next several generations,
at least, there can be no question of finding some other body
of knowledge to substitute for what we now have. Few if any
of today's leading figures of the "knowledge industry"
would even take seriously the question of alternative fields of

knowledge, although they might admit that a century hence what we viewed as knowledge in the 1970s would by then have been relegated to no more than the status of a historical anachronism.

Nevertheless, for our contemporary and near-future purposes there remains the problem of the unsuitability of traditional learning as the sole basis for the formal education of our youth. We are, further, abusing this tradition by restricting the uses to which we do put it. We are maintaining it as *inert* knowledge and, worse still, we are trying to transmit it as equally inert, so that it ends by serving us very poorly indeed. Thus, the problem is not one of ridding ourselves of this tradition of knowledge but of conveying it more meaningfully, in a context suited to the times and to the student's present and future requirements. The issue has to do with *how* rather than with *what:* by what means do we best provide the student with a sufficient grasp of extant knowledge so that he can use it in an environmental quest — to adapt and grow?

We continue to maintain the traditional learning in forms no longer appropriate to today's conditions. More bluntly stated, we insist on an adult-centered, administratively convenient learning situation, thereby derogating youth and its learning impulse at the very time when support is most needed. Roles of both learner and guide are confused. The place of the adult guide in the formal learning process has tended to congeal into that of a repetitious trainer (not unlike the animal trainer in a circus) and that of the learner into a respondent who (if we extend the metaphor, like a circus animal) is required to behave on cue but in his animal perversity often acts on impulse and embarrasses his trainer. The school setting is remote from social reality, even that of the local scene; learners see no reason for the tasks they are made to carry out, and they burn away their energies in fighting what they view as an inexplicable and willful imposition of authority in the organization of learning activities. Everyone cries out for change. But change of what kind and in what direction?

A new tradition is gradually emerging, one more suited to environmental adaptation via formal schooling. But it will, even as it accepts the worth of the old learning, lead to establishment of drastic new canons of operation. It will require our viewing the body of traditional learning as a means, not an end. It will downgrade the old, overly formalized teacher-pupil relationship and break down other interpersonal barriers to communication within the learning milieu. By a restructuring of the learning environment it will place more of the burden of learning upon the learner, doing so more fairly than in the past through an emphasis on the social motivations that come naturally to the individual who works in a group. These are serious and far-reaching fundamental changes, not to be accepted easily.

In summary, I may state that any tradition, to continue serving a functional purpose in society, cannot be allowed to ossify: it must be reshaped to fit emerging new needs. The work of Piaget suggests a growing gap between the young child's need for an education that balances moral and cognitive experience and the capability of today's formal system of elementary education to provide that balanced experience. This gap widens as the child enters the period of adolescence, with its stringent demands for behavior more in conformity with adult norms. Ill prepared to find meaning in learning through his elementary school background, the typical youth finds junior and senior high school education dull, frustrating, unreasonably competitive, and unrelated to what he holds at the time to be the realities of existence. He develops, unfortunately, a mental set against the reflective life, against nonexploitative modes of living, against the institutions of society for challenging his impulsive behavior. The school becomes his prime symbol of pointless social constraint. Instead of providing him with formative experience in line with his future needs, it tends to turn him against those very states of mind and modes of behavior which could serve those needs. It does not prepare him to enter adult life on terms of relative advantage but instead leaves him at a greater disadvantage as he emerges into the complications of life in adult society.

Traditional learning in its pure form, therefore, more and more ceases to serve the essential purposes of young people, who must look forward to adult life in an environmentalized social order. Youth has a positive power of complaint over its situation, but it has no power to enforce change. Only society, through its ruling elites, is able to mandate necessary change. Schools, representing as they presently do, the traditional forces of restraint much more than the cutting edge of change in society, exist in a state of entropy. Disjunction cannot continue endlessly, however, either in a biological or a social organism. Again, the question of change must be faced: since there is to be change and since we can expect in some measure to control it, what should be the substance of that change and in what direction should it take us?

On the operational plane this means a reconsideration of the basis for behavior change through schooling. Should hereditary factors, differences in natural capability among different individuals and groups, be seriously considered in mapping out new paths to follow? Can the human learning potential itself be developed fast enough and far enough to make adaptation more a reality than a still-distant dream? What shapes might a new, "environmental" school of tomorrow assume? To these questions we turn next.

6

Nature, Nurture, and the Environmental School of Tomorrow

Definitions of learning nowadays almost invariably include some mention of "change in behavior" expected as an outcome of the learning process. Certainly the ability of an individual to alter his patterns of behavior is of significance in any society. It marks the line of differentiation between possessors of intelligence and those who do not possess it. Use of the ability brings about a "change in human disposition or capability, which can be retained, and which is not simply ascribable to the process of growth."[1] This evidence of capacity, or its absence in appropriate circumstances, must be by any form of measurement a significant determinant of how well new behavior patterns can be acquired.

Another important element, however, must be reckoned with. This is heredity. The continuing nature-nurture controversy has kept in the forefront of scholars' attention the question of what relative effects inheritance exerts, in contrast to the effects of an organism's surroundings, on a

138

subject's behavior and development. The suspicion that hereditary influences may act to impose particular upper limits upon any individual's learning (and hence, behavioral) capabilities, although wildly indulged at the time of the Jensen imbroglio, has still not been fairly laid to rest.[2]

As man faces the reality of a limited environment and that of his own inadequacies in adjusting to that environment, these considerations take on a new dimension of significance. We face the unpleasant fact that mass social behavior must eventually be assessed in terms of outcome within both the earthly support system and human society itself. The incredible difficulty of prescribing "environmental" modes of behavior for a mass society poses for the social thinker not only pragmatic questions of supply and demand or of how social services can be maintained at appropriate levels but also questions of value and of ultimate goals for humanity. Practically all literate people with a social conscience feel anxiety over issues of both types. Yet how many have been able to reduce their uncertain musings to something objective, to at least the suggestion of a formula that might engender in new generations that "environmental" behavior without which human life will presumably continue steadily to deteriorate?

One aspect of the problem is the assumption of affluence as an indefinitely persisting phenomenon, once a society has achieved a suitable level of development. An opposite view (i.e., that riches may be little more than an accident of history and a temporary as well as mixed blessing) has the superior virtue of allowing one to account more reasonably for the fact that even today only a tiny percentage of the earth's population, after hundreds of years of socioeconomic development, enjoys a significant standard of wealth. And it should hardly be overlooked that those few societies which have amassed wealth in the contemporary period have no assurance that they will be able to luxuriate indefinitely in possession of their riches. Further, wealth is seemingly not an unmitigated good. Orthodox Marxism may or may not be correct in the contention that capitalism in its more unregenerate form always rests on a base of mass poverty. Yet even as they have eliminated or drastically reduced poverty the few rich nations have been relatively unable to stem the flood of other evils that wealth apparently brings to a contemporary mass society.

So long as an advanced social order retains a relative freedom from the need to rationalize resource use down to every last square foot of land or shock of wheat, the society may permit behavior rather widely divergent from that which the laws of parsimony ordinarily dictate. But always such a society must reckon with other, less-obvious costs. When nature provides barriers to resource availability or limits resource use by refusing to absorb pollution caused by uncontrolled consumption, then social forces must tend to converge in enforcing conformity to a standard of behavior more in line with the laws of parsimony. The movement of environmentalism cannot help exerting this effect, sooner or later, on human behavior; its compulsions may indeed prove stronger than those of any more artificial agent of parsimony (e.g., Communism), for the reason that its application presupposes not only that worldly wealth be spread more equitably through society but that human behavior must conform more closely to the unavoidable limitations set by nature herself.

How will the social evolution of man, in a few brief decades, bring about the more balanced mass behavior that a dawning environmental age requires? Heredity and learning will both be involved as this transcending development in human affairs moves to center stage. The following observations represent one view of how this phase of late twentieth-century history may unfold.

Heredity and Environmental Behavior

Charles Darwin, in chapter 4 of *Origin of Species,* states: "It may metaphorically be said that natural selection is daily and hourly scrutinising, throughout the world, the slightest variations; rejecting those that are bad, preserving and adding up those that are good; silently and insensibly working, *whenever and wherever opportunity offers,* at the improvement of each organic being in relation to its organic and inorganic conditions of life."[3] This statement would have the same general validity today as in 1859, except that for humans and a good many other species the number of unavoidable stimuli requiring adaptive response has multiplied phenomenally. As the pace of change and development in our post-industrial era increases in greater than geometrical progression, forcing upon humanity the kind of intricate web of pressures that a century ago could not have been imagined, the slow, unseen process of progressive adaptation consonant with Darwin's thinking becomes a victim of the speeded-up tempo of contemporary existence. Opportunity for nature to mold its adaptive physiological process to an appropriate time scheme is effectively destroyed. A child born today can expect to experience by the time he reaches the age of twenty perhaps a half million more response-demanding stimulus situations than would a child born in 1873 during the comparable age span — but both would have possessed substantially the same physical equipment, and the differences between the two in responsive psychic capacity could all too easily be exaggerated.

Heredity is manifested in a complex design of desirable and undesirable outcomes. But overshadowing other aspects of inheritance is the problem of time lag: man cannot breed himself into a more disease-resistant organism in time to avoid the more serious physical disasters of a technological way of life. "Nearly all the health problems have been created by or intensified by our modern technology and affluent society. Never have people had an environment so good and so bad."[4]

Even discounting the bodily effects of living under the amounts of stress which are now considered normal, a human species that could live successfully for a prolonged period with atmospheric conditions such as those which occurred in

Donora, Pennsylvania, in 1948,[5] is not likely to emerge. Of course, the permanent use of gas masks and other mechanical aids to body maintenance may be considered. But such inhibiting practices break down the "natural" sense of free life that any organism inherits and normally maintains. Generations would have to pass before these practices of artificially sustaining life were adjusted to psychically as well as physically.

The point is that man's rate of adaptation to whatever difficulties technological life imposes cannot be speeded up through normal hereditary processes. Natural selection assumes a new aspect in a world characterized by such swift and unrelenting change in the environment but in which there is no change in the human body and its reproductive functions. Perhaps man has thus far succeeded in adapting as well as might be expected. But unfortunately his burdens are tending to mount rather than diminish. His frail body and no less frail mind show resilience, but still there are more breakdowns than can be considered acceptable. Statisticians tell us that mental illness in today's advanced societies exists in a degree never before known in all of history.

There are two possible avenues of solution: first, to alter in dramatically meliorative terms the physical environment man inhabits; or, second, to speed up artificially, through manipulated heredity, the process of natural selection. The first alternative is in large part untenable; man's technology can only in some degree be better controlled; it cannot be done away with. The second alternative, which as yet appears to involve dangers greater than society as a whole is prepared to face, nevertheless presents intriguing possibilities, not only to the science-fiction enthusiast but also to *bona fide* scientists.

Scientific breeding of humans could, under appropriate circumstances and given social sanction, speed up the entire evolutionary process. Apart from matters of sociomoral inhibition, a fair case for deliberate programming of genetic outcomes can be made. Science has demonstrated in the development of domestic animals the extent to which planning produces the kinds of useful creatures men require. Naturally, we cannot suppose that all the [plant and animal] breeds were suddenly produced as perfect and as useful as we now see them; indeed, in many cases, we know that this has not been their history. The key is man's power of accumulative selection: nature gives successive variations; man adds them up in certain directions useful to him. In this sense he may be said to have made for himself useful breeds. The great power of this principle of selection is not hypothetical.[6]

Planned human reproduction could serve to eliminate undesirable genes from the genetic pool. It would within certain limits do away with the problem of physically and mentally defective children, now more than ever a *social* problem. It would allow parents to mate with decisions already, in effect, successfully made with regard to a child's sex, physical characteristics, and intelligence level. Most significantly, it would have the potential, if applied as a part of a society-wide, fully accepted plan for total social development, achieve what (as was suggested previously) cannot now be done — speed up the rate of adaptation by speeding up the work of the selective principle.

Against these claims there may be raised a number of strong counterarguments. By such a resort to inbreeding to produce superior types, the hybrid vigor that today's random mating insures will be lost. Further, an abnormally long interval, even given the best of luck, must occur between initiation of the policy of genetic planning and its extension through all generations and social groupings (e.g., racial, class). During this interval a superrace will be emerging, while a hybrid race will be facing elimination: violence under these circumstances could hardly be avoided. And finally, over the whole question lingers the profound issue of moral right. Can one wonder at the acerbic reactions this matter of genetic planning arouses?

Criteria of potential adaptive success, in fact, are extremely difficult to locate in the genetic context. Controversy over the supposed differential contributions of race to human adaptation provides a case in point. The well-known Pro-

fessor Shockley addressed these words to a meeting of the
American Psychological Association:

> If those Negroes with the fewest Caucasian genes are . . . the most
> prolific and also the least intelligent, then genetic enslavement will
> be the destiny of their next generation. The consequences may be
> extremes of racism for both blacks and whites.[7]

Citing a study of 122 pairs of identical twins, this adherent
of genetic activism concludes that heredity is the major
factor in intelligence and therefore "the major deficit in
Negro intellectual performance must be primarily of hereditary
origin."[8] Yet Shockley's prescriptions (e.g., a "voluntary,
sterilization bonus plan," in which a thousand dollars would
be paid for every I.Q. point below 100 to a person submit-
ting to voluntary sterilization[9]) clearly escalate extremism
in the genetic conflict. Insistence on such forced-draft
measures, no less than possible use of sperm banks among
social classes already predominant socioeconomically, suggests inevitable violent confrontation with all its attendant
uncertainties and risk.

As with race, so with other variables linked primarily to
heredity. National origin, sex, family social or financial
status, or even legitimacy of birth tend to provide sources
for social judgments of the individual *a priori*. They con-
found the issue by introducing environmental considerations.
One cannot state with certainty that a Negro child with an
I.Q., say, in the 110-115 range would not achieve intellectually at the level of a comparable white child if raised in a
milieu exactly like that of the white child. One cannot claim
with any assurance that a female child of I.Q. 112 would not
succeed as well as a male child of that I.Q. if the circumstances of their development were similar. We are dealing here
with the problem of limited controls in the comparison of
environmental effects. The idiosyncratic character of each
human being's conditions of life suggests that the effects of

heredity cannot for the forseeable future be pinpointed well enough to permit acceptance outside narrow cliques of "true believers" of formulae such as Shockley's, or even the more subtle and qualified conclusions of Arthur Jensen. Without the ability to turn his power of selection, as yet, to the betterment of his own species, and to do it safely, man has no choice for the immediate future but to follow the natural evolutionary path of development, slow and inappropriate as that may be in the circumstances. It seems reasonable to suggest that on this path, since breeding is uncontrolled and the imperfectly endowed or motivated appear as frequently as do more "suitable" types, the key to human survival must be principally learning: not merely the capacity to ingest abstract data, but an ongoing, constantly adaptive use of received data to remake the individual into a totality greater that the sum of his separate parts. This learning is by definition environmental in nature. It links man with his world and it provides the only secure motive for his engaging in a basic compact with the society he inhabits: a compact that implicitly states both his own and his society's responsibilities in achieving a *human* coexistence with the physical universe supporting all.

Learning and Environmental Behavior

The term *expert society*[10] has been coined to suggest a strong trend in advanced technological societies toward an increasing reward value placed upon "know-how" or technical expertise in management or industrial specialism. There is also a valuable "know-how" required, especially by the state,[11] in determining how and when judgments of social utility or aesthetic preference should be made. Expertise in these and other areas cannot be acquired in a vacuum. Formal education has become more than ever in man's past a lever to use in prying open the otherwise blocked avenues to career progress. Overt symbols of subject-field mastery such as advanced degrees are at this late date essential prerequisites to advancement in one's work or in his level of remuneration.

There is a definite element of social growth in this radical dissemination of expertness through the higher intellectual layers of advanced societies. Service occupations represent by far the greatest single area of job expansion in such societies. The dedicated search by whole new classes of "workers" in intellectual or technological pursuits for better ways of serving humanity in the mass and individually has become one of the newer standard life patterns. Men like heart transplant surgeons or the social welfare workers who daily enter Harlem or Watts accept the necessity of service above gain in a sense that would be meaningless to, say, the old-fashioned military mind or the Babbitt-like unregenerate money-manager mind. A knowledge of accomplishment and a feeling of satisfaction accompany work thus performed so that, whatever its challenges, the work itself provides the pleasure that others must seek in sex or liquor or watching television. Yet expertness has other dimensions even than this most important element of the new level of work satisfaction.

Learning is needed, we may say, to produce the expert, the technically competent member of an expert society. But it is possible that, under circumstances not too difficult to imagine, the person who has developed this technical competence through learning may be fixated at the technical/manipulative level. American society today, with all its successful management of technology, seems to contain an extraordinary number of men and women who, while they literally thrive on business competition and the stimulation of professional contacts, appear in their personal and social development to be somewhat stunted. This condition within society may be measured not only by the rising financial success of psychiatrists as an occupational group but also by the range of patently destructive actions (obviously preceded by equally destructive thoughts) of these same business and professional people in their private lives.

Learning in these cases has been suspended at a certain point in the process; the learning is incomplete, has not been used as the tool by which to further self-development; the individual to that degree has failed to realize any significant integration of himself with the outer universe of changing forms and shapes of experience. This blockage of learning has defeated essential purposes of individual and environmental enhancement, although it may have been, from the narrowly individual point of view, precisely the element that permitted the achievement of ego-diverting, limited social purposes. One might say with William James that "our hour of triumph is what brings the void."

Another needed level of "expertness" is suggested by this condition, a level more consistent with full human potential for learning and adaptation. True, this higher level of functioning may be bound up with man's effort to hurry psychological evolution. The latter may be no more susceptible to force-feeding than is biological evolution. The social friction caused by pressures in this direction may be quite out of proportion to the costs incurred. However, there are grounds for believing that such a development not only is inevitable (since man must grow individually as well as socially, while the two forms of growth are not always mutually reinforcing) but may also prove to be the ultimate necessity, *because man must govern himself better* if he is to survive in an environment capable of no more than a specifiable, limited degree of exploitation.

Of what would this higher "expertness" consist, then? For the individual, it will mean — for those who possess a suitable base in inherited capacities — the continuous, lifelong cultivation of self-governance in the interest of adaptive, idiosyncratic behavior. It is obvious that full development of the self, within only the limits that a particular form of social life prescribes, must be the complement of such behavior; it is the natural line of *personal* development toward which an environmental mode of behavior leads. The person would achieve a level of development for which expertise in some specialized line of work and appropriate social skills would provide the obvious guarantee, although it could not be expected to occur inevitably merely because such abilities had been demonstrated. Admittedly, development at so high a level cannot in the first instance be expected of many in the mass society. This is not the problem in an evolutionary sense. More important is the creation of modes of social intercourse that will carry a zest for self-development beyond purely intellectual concerns and utilize the masses' reservoir of talents for coping and adjusting, to give them also motives for valuing and developing the self over and above the trials of daily life.

This means, in effect, devising shatterproof personalities, a challenge as much to the individual person in all his uniqueness as to the organizing and inventive powers of the present leadership class in the technological society. The many individual disappointments of personal life in a time of increasing competition for worldly advantage must be reckoned with. Some old as well as some fairly new assumptions will require reexamination. Maslow's needs theory, for example, which posits that, in general, "higher-order" needs for self-actualization can be met only if "lower-order" needs have first been gratified, may have little application to newly emerging patterns of social life. It may also overlook vital human-adjustment possibilities that no theory has yet recognized. Assumptions of anterior need appear to break down when one examines the cases of POW behavior, it may be noted. "Ordinary" men, as prisoners, were denied all but the most elemental requirements (food, water) yet, without any of their so-called lower-order needs fulfilled, the majority of these men persisted in meeting their experience with openness, self-reserve, and belief in their strength to endure. Is their predicament, then, a model of the 1984 social torture chamber in which all must live? Are they, then, prototypes of future, "environmentalized" humanity?

Recognition of environmental limitations must play a crucial role in successful futurist behavior, obviously. Such behavior, to the degree in which it is genuinely environmental, is an extension into time, space, and social consciousness of the most irreducible moral learning. But psychological wholeness of any organism is a matter of attainable balance — between the organism and the milieu within which it behaves. Freudian, behaviorist, and more recently the Maslow "Third Force" theories of behavior all tend to focus on the individual as much or more than on limitations in the milieu. They take for granted a basic, undeniable amount of "elbow room" in which an individual organism can express its self-aggrandizing behavior. It has not been sufficiently remarked how much the organized societies of today have already restricted that "elbow room" to mental as opposed to physical fields of maneuver. The crowning achievement of this trend may well be the standard paperback novel, with its glut of vicarious conquests, sexual, social, political, and so on, by a hero who remains happily content with a common man's anti-intellectual outlook. The reader's needs for self-acceptance at the expense of his physical and social environment are probably increased rather than satisfied by experiences such as this. As with violence on television, the social outcomes of such soaking of the imagination in dreams that can never be are of doubtful value.

It may be, as Lorenz suggests, that we all-too-easily over-stress *any* learning as the product of milieu, when actually it has its provenance in biological causality. "For instance, the belief that human aggression is based not on phylogenetic adaptation but on learning implies a tremendous under-assessment of its dangers. Hitherto this belief has only led to the production of thousands of intolerably aggressive non-frustrated children, but it may lead to much worse things."[12] Thus, one must remain aware of the risk of simple explanations of events that are produced by a complexity of causes.

Nevertheless, when the satisfaction of so many apparent needs for individuals coping in an aggressive way against the forces of a complicated culture has the effect of increasing competition and thus making one's own freedom contingent upon another's nonfreedom, the social consequences to that culture must be weighed. Expressive behavior that blocks another's behavior may produce a momentary sense of ascendancy or security, but its more important outcome is conflict. While exact instances of such situations might be spelled out at great length, the point for any student of contemporary and future social life should be clear without further elaboration: the measure of a functional social system must be, given human and natural limitations, its capability for minimizing the buildup of more interpersonal conflict than can be accommodated under current conditions of group existence. Therefore inversion of the drive for personal security, so that the individual always seeks to find a more vital security by turning more deeply into himself, becomes the only alternative to the patently bankrupt policy of placing the locus of security within an exploitable thing or person, something outside the individual. This dictum has wide ramifications for social and personal life in the dawning environmental era. Regardless of how it might be defined in terms of single situations, its direction is clear: it leads to yet another search, one more challenging than any heretofore undertaken — for the unique, new expertness required for survival in post-industrial life.

The Social-Evolutionary Character of
Environmental Learning

The race for what is thought to be security has led men in the mass to focus narrowly on temporary goals. Compulsion in behavior and a blind search for predictibility of results are the fruits of this narrow focus. Domination over other animals and over the material world has shifted the locus of conflict without diminishing its intensity. Where once there was conflict between man on the one hand and beasts and natural forces on the other, now we see also conflict among groups of humans, within each group, between individuals, and within the single individual himself. Looking back upon the technological achievements of the twentieth century to this point, we might well assert that man's undeniable domination of all other life forms and of the physical environment represents really only a partial accomplishment, a way-station on the road to some more distant, still-sought goal.

In the simplistic view that first thoughts of the new quest for adaptation evoke, there is an emphasis on purification, purging the race once and for all of its atavisms and excesses. This view appeals to the one-level mind, the joiner or out-and-out reformer. It is made to order for the mentality whose avidity for formula solutions and mass causes was so well described in Eric Hoffer's *The True Believer*. Instead, however, sober judgment bids us waste little time with such oversimplifications and seek a rationale better suited to the complex conditions of the times.

One point seems clear. The challenge of symbiosis that mass psychological evolution presents rejects all insistence on making any change that further widens the gap between the average man and that assorted group of intellectuals, high-society lights, technocrats, and their camp followers who may be said to form a current elite or meritocracy. Rather, society must undertake to develop newer and more socially adaptive bridges to every individual, high or low in status, bridges of humanity. Nor can there be any substitute for *critical* individuality of behavior in a society moving toward third-phase sociopsychological evolution.

> Nothing is more superficial than a global condemnation of mass culture and its content. One must oppose to this rejection a critical attitude that frees cultural innovation from the social control that weighs it down. Just as in the last century some totally rejected industrialization, only criticism of its social control and of the uses to which it was put led to the formation of social movements and social change.[13]

This innovation, which can free a culture from the deadening impact of retrogressive social control while individual adaptations in its direction can be developed effectively and on a discrete basis, unfortunately cannot easily be packaged for mass teaching and learning. It constitutes an indirect process in the mass, hence its difficulty. Those who will be led must not, in a large measure, become aware of the fact that they are led. What teaching can be accomplished at this stage would require the solution of certain pedagogic problems associated with the present "system" of processing learning in formal settings. There is also the question of how informal learning can be utilized toward the end of innovative mass behavior. But even in advance of all this, and the point is crucial, public goals policy must, however roughly, be determined. Since an actual voting procedure on so complex an issue can in no wise be envisioned at this stage of social development, a goals policy requires that leadership set the direction. Waiting for the public to voice its will would be tantamount to abdication of all leadership responsibility. As in any other truly evolutionary development, a vanguard movement must exist and it must be involved during a lead-time period in critical initial phases of adaptation.

Individuality will require a new working definition, socially and psychologically, as this process gathers momentum. This is the adaptive antidote, the social-survival *sine qua non,* for a social order that on the purely operational side faces an anti-individual trend too powerful for any degree of successful, overt resistance — toward ever more effective and value-drained social and economic rationalization of all physical and most psychic human activity. It is not merely a question of promoting more people into wringing a greater payoff from their private efforts at personal development; this must also occur within a context of parallel diminishing returns from old-style individualism in both individual *and* social terms. Society can no longer afford the freedom-loving, wenching jackanapes of earlier and happier times, not because it cannot admire him and his worry-free animal behavior, but because *his* freedom has become society's straitjacket.

In broad terms one may describe man as being driven

irreversibly, by the flow of events that he has already had a strong hand in shaping through history, toward that condition of existence in which more and more of his animal and autistic urges are positively circumscribed, leaving him only the alternative path of psychological self-development. For the future this development dovetails with environmental needs, social and geophysical. Patterns of adaptation, enforced by conditions reflecting this trend, will shift the nature of the individual's response. Failure to respond adequately and in time will predispose individuals to early bypassing in the struggle for fulfilled existence. A new type of man with new capabilities is reaching the fore.

As that emerging truth comes to be better recognized, its implications for policy can be more fully assessed. Society's once primary functions, namely, providing an individual with a reference group within which "normal" life can go on, socializing the person to the constraints of group life, and the like, are undergoing slow but steady erosion. This is seen in the friction generated by its institutions. The latter, inherited from an earlier, less crowded and complex time, serve now, even among the better classes, more a policing than a maintenance purpose, and in the affluent nations, with their cohorts of well-educated but socially unintegrated youth, such institutions are most reviled by the very groups and individuals they most securely support.

Society is out of phase. As Drucker explains it, society in industrial nations has reached the "end of continuity."[14] The new requirements laid upon people bring reactions of frustration vented upon outdated social institutions. Yet the institutions cannot be discarded and replaced by other models, assuming scientists could devise them, without dependable individuals in large numbers to make the new institutions work. Progress waits upon the emergence of new social understandings. This is the same as saying that the race will and must change, also that evolutionary change will succeed in altering man unquestionably in the direction of environmental adaptation. Yet this evolution, however inevitable, is not guaranteed to proceed according to any predetermined timetable. And while it may occur relatively painlessly, it may more likely involve trauma and disorder. It depends finally upon the thoughts and actions of individuals, singly and in combination.

Society, Learning, and Sane
Environmental Behavior

In the work of major psychologists of learning, whatever the theoretical framework implied, there is a a disturbing tendency to seek proof of any theory by investigation of discrete learning phenomena. Gagné, for example, is much concerned with learning chains,[15] Skinner with reinforcement contingencies,[16] and Ausubel with subsumption of detail into a core of knowledge already in the subject's possession.[17] The problem here is not that behavioral scientists fail to present holistic theories into which their individual observations fit. It is, rather, that these theories tend too much only to account for consistent performances. That is, they account for sequences of behavior involving some forms of behavior repetition, either of single, totally discrete actions or of combinations in a recognizable aspect. They do *not* account in any comprehensive sense for the typical continuum of performances by a human being in a situation (e.g., "real life") *in which no artificial or constant structure of behavioral constraints can be imposed.* It is therefore impossible to generalize from these theories to apply them to the very basis of behavior, namely that of individuals freely acting on thought and impulse in a mass social setting, which is of most significance to the environmental thinker.

Predictability of behavior, in short, cannot be limited to largely laboratory situations if it is to have meaning for environmental purposes. Reductionist and simplistic ideals of learning will result, obviously, from too literal a generalization from any theory stressing laboratory controls. This is perhaps most apparent in the transfer of Skinner's principles from controlled to free behavioral situations. Where a subject faces a choice among multiple ways of behaving and cannot envision a manageable handful of possible outcomes, the theory of operant conditoning is likely to prove much divorced from its practice. The average classroom teaching-learning situation leads to a failure of learning, for example, for two related reasons: 1) an assumption of predictibility and of appropriate conditioning has been incorrectly made; 2) a social climate suitable to individual and group motivation has never been established.

The idea of conditioning is never in itself unsuitable to the promotion of specific forms of learning. Conditioning can always help — or hinder. What has to be understood is how it shall be applied to the learning situation when socially grounded behavior already acts to undermine many alternative approaches to instruction. Conditioning of a specific and limited kind cannot very well take place successfully in the presence of counterconditioning elements that are not only uncomprehended but, worse still, ignored or not even recognized.

Even so, if one looks upon the classroom or school as a mirror of the larger social world outside, one will observe that influences from outside permeate the formal learning situation and can be made use of in ways that do conceivably serve an environmental purpose. Conditioning can hardly be shrugged off as unsuited to achievement of such a purpose, either, when we realize how difficult it is for a majority of youth in a palpably treacherous milieu to subject all issues and problems to methods of dialectic that seem to serve the young, in their inexperience, so inadequately.

A type of conditioning is already acting to enforce "environment" and in the same moment to break down "anti-environment" in the community and, by extension, in the school. This may be seen in the "new" television commercials, stressing a more restrained way of life, aimed at both direct and subliminal effect just as, ironically, earlier commercials and others still being aired stress a life of abandon and discreet vice. Especially for the young this approach *does* engender learning, however banal it may seem to the intellectually developed mind. Even more ambitious, and specifically directed toward enforcement of attitude change in an educational setting, of course, is the growing ideology of "environmentalizing" schooling itself.

In one of its forms this ideology seeks to sensitize through increasing the child's awareness. This can take on a somewhat openly didactic rather that a more subtly sensitizing aspect. One author cites several of the fundamental problems of "environmental misunderstanding" (i.e., lack of awareness, lack of concern, lack of competence, substantive misinformation, and hypocrisy).[18] He then goes on to assert a need to saturate classrooms and schools with environmental purpose, employing every available tool, extending over the complete range of stimuli for learning, including the subject matter of the separate fields of knowledge, to make students continually thoughtful in their reaction to environmental imperatives.[19] The purpose here is comprehensiveness, but essentially didactic, and even propagandistic methods dominate.

Another approach suggests the need for change within the curriculum itself before learning will eventuate in appropriate response capability. It is "essential that a systematized curriculum be developed. Such a curriculum should include environmental perceptions developed in a progressively complex nature, with concepts and activities expanded in a horizontal learning manner as well as in a vertical plane."[20] Both these expositions are typical of the present state of thinking on formal environmental education, and certainly constitute progress of a sort over, say, the situation in schools a decade ago, when environmental concerns hardly entered the formal curriculum at all.

Yet these developments cannot help creating as much dissatisfaction as achievement under present circumstances. They lack a social philosophical base. They are tied to the rationalist-perfectionist concept of man inherited from the Enlightenment, a concept that tends too much toward the belief in and dependence on intellectually exercised controls as sufficient to cure all human ills. The unrealism of such approaches is measured by their total dependence on intellectual *receiving* as well as intellectual planning of learning experiences that will produce appropriate behavioral response. They do not arise out of a vision of what man's changed conditions of life in future time will make of *him*, socially and morally. The tired old assumption that objective knowledge brings freedom and that such knowledge can be made available to *all* becomes useless in a still-developing mass society. The need for suitable conditioning experiences for the greater percentage of those nearly four billion souls already inhabiting the earth could not have become more totally apparent than by considering such well-intentioned but too openly didactic approaches to "environmentalization" of the school experience. The question, then, is not one of achieving for society in the mass the intellectual's "freedom" of awareness or of objective knowledge. Instead, it is that of changing the overall direction of mass-conditioned behavior. Extending outward through cognitive awareness, the vector of effective environmental behavior thus becomes in reality an allied and supporting feature of environmental education. The intellectual function in experience, when it can reasonably be cultivated, buttresses the conditioning function; it does not replace it. These two must be developed in tandem, in fact, even in educating a potential elite.

   That it is in society's better interest to seek improved environmental behavior has already been demonstrated in the America of the 1970s, where public policy has evolved considerably toward acceptance of the principle of measuring consequences of exploitative commercial activity (e.g., continued despoilment of the land through outdated mining practices) against overall socioeconomic gains. But this is only one aspect of environmentalism. Society in its governance of the learning process will come increasingly to recognize that sane environmental behavior does not apply solely to decisions made in corporate boardrooms. It has to do with the sum total of human actions, and the philosophy of environmentalism pinpoints for criticism that behavior of individuals which involves unfair exploitation, not only of the earth and its envelope of surrounding air but of all animal life inhabiting the planet, including other humans. In coming to understand this essential and difficult truth, people will also come to appreciate how inadequate the bulky and rigid body of inherited laws must be to a complex future, how environmental justice must of necessity take on forms different from those of contemporary legalistic justice. Patently society faces the need to learn much that is new and more relevant; it needs to learn how to govern itself in an environmental sense.

Toward an Educational Alternative

What are the ground rules of human behavior that ought to concern us at this point in our search? Most important, no effort should be spared to speak freely about the human adjustment status. That status has probably come about, even if one cannot unravel the historical skein of causes and effects that has led us to today, because men in the mass were unable to resist various forms of social suggestion and/or coercion shaping their behavior. In short, they were conditioned.

Conditioning an organism's behavior can take many forms, but the conditioned behavior should have an effect of leading the organism (as psychologists tell us) toward homeostasis. One organism will react to the environment in a different way from another in seeking this state of internal balance. Social conditions can determine to some degree how organisms react to stimuli. [21] Men in the mass, it is reasonably safe to say, have a socially strengthened (and of course biologically based) tendency to behave exploitatively toward elements of their environment such as food, machines, and other humans. Conditioning, whatever its causes and their complexity, has led to predictable results: when objects of use are available, the average man will demonstrate exploitative behavior; when such objects are unavailable, he will adopt some alternate behavior pattern (a show of frustration, of acceptance, of total nonreaction, transfer of interest to some other object that is available).

In today's developed societies, with their interdependence of a market economy and with a large percentage of the population conditioned to a high standard of living, an inordinate, unrealistic emphasis on consumer privilege, founded on an erroneous belief in the continuous availability of resources, dominates public thinking and behavior. Government tends to sidestep the social implications of an equation whose terms are constantly drifting further out of balance. The social problems that this imbalance brings about are becoming, by the late 1970s, more apparent, and their international implications more formidable.

We are by tradition tied to a historical creed of conservative liberalism, rooted initially in Enlightenment social theory, which holds that physical resources will always match or exceed human demand and that the possessors of affluence can always, with suitable assistance from government as a benign intermediary, redistribute wealth to a degree sufficient to maintain socioeconomic balance and popular cooperation with the powers that be. The experience of both the Western democracies (notably in North America and Western Europe) and the Soviet Union, which has hardly, at any time in six decades of Marxist-Leninist rule, adequately fulfilled the promise of "enough for all" implicit in fundamental Marxian doctrine, seems to show positively that society has a very long way to travel before the erroneous assumptions of inevitable affluence and of natural limits on the growth of popular demand can be laid to rest. Yet the neo-Malthusian, creeping famine of the 1970s in many parts of the underdeveloped world must surely suggest how tenuous is man's hold over the necessities of existence, to say nothing of the superfluous luxuries.

What must government's role be in developing administrative and educational policy to meet the social problems of mistaken affluence? Time-marking or caretaker governments are surely courting trouble by failing to accept the problem in its longer-term ramifications. The complexity of relationships among individuals and institutions in a society undergoing steady democratization may bring about increasing ineffectiveness of not only existing, traditional forms of legal administration of justice but also of the system for distribution of primary economic goods, whenever such methods of fulfilling human needs fail to conform to the reality of social evolution. There is an ever-present danger that government will, with enough consistency, misread the advance directions of change and thus fail to act in time to maintain minimal social order. The results could be catastrophic.

That society has the right to condition neophyte members against such a ubiquitous evil as the mass assumption of abundance can never be acknowledged automatically. This right must be purchased in coin from those classes in society which have a vested interest in continuing that assumption. More than this, a corps of socially realistic change agents must be activated for the purpose of charting a turnaround in policy and dealing with a host of still only vaguely discerned post-turnaround problems. This whole process is made all the more difficult by the success of the mass conditioning that has produced the existing situation. Initially, progress must consist in perhaps nothing more than the airing of questions that a few years ago would have been taken as foolish.

Beyond this, there is a need to explore a *variety* of ways and means of counterconditioning. The consumer society has now been conditioned so thoroughly to its role of buying on impulse, of on-cue laughter in the television studio, and similar prescribed social responses that one is thought to be aberrant or antisocial to suggest that such behavior is of dubious value to both the individual and society. Therefore, rather than dwell on the public's right to stagnate indefinitely in its existing web of conditioned behavior, it becomes a matter of some profit to turn to those avenues by which the mass psyche can be counterconditioned without the *angst* and opposition that a direct, obvious turnaround will produce.

Awareness is not universal and never will be. It is a particular capability of a fairly small proportion of mankind lucky enough to have been placed in a position of developing and using the powers of intellect to increase control over the self within a given milieu. Certainly for the masses *now living,* the approximation of third-stage psychological evolution is unattainable. People must be helped to finish out their existence without destroying the minority of intellectual activists already at work constructing the foundations of a new society. Education is the key to success in this task, but not an education primarily for awareness.

Our contemporary schools are successful in one area of functioning, and an unquestioned success at that: they inculcate the desire for self-development within that percentage of learners which has an affinity for academic and reflective pursuits as its natural birthright. Beyond this, the schools are relative failures. They not only attempt to promote this manner of learning among a majority of students, for whom this mode of approach is quite unsuited; they also eschew any responsibility for counterconditioning by which to reverse behavior that for the individual is ego-destroying and for society environmentally catastrophic. For the indefinite future, until the point of substantive educational change is reached, a majority of all school-aged youth will probably be forced to endure a profitless experience, inevitably "turned off" by bookishness and bookish people and by enforced reflection. Society has the burden not of withholding education from these young people but of providing the kind of education that they need and that the world of tomorrow must have.

Schools are institutions well able to reinforce counterconditioning once that process has been initiated. By themselves, however, schools can do little to begin or carry on a process of this kind. They require aid and vast moral support from the outside. At present they tend to show, in their inability to hold the so-called nonacademic students, that traditional learning, organized as it has been for centuries past, has no more than a limited pedagogic utility. But radical school reorganization still lies in the future, and this for the reason that society has not yet comprehended its own role in that reorganization. Schools, it seems clear, cannot do the work of which they are capable in building a more adaptable people unless (or until) a meaningful collaboration with other social elements can be arranged. Fortunately, events appear to be moving advanced societies somewhat in the direction of such collaboration.

To appreciate the magnitude of this issue one must also appreciate the difficulty of individual life in an age of social complexity. Dissonance within the individual psyche, as the work of the Freudian school as well as that of more recent psychologists tends to show, builds up inner conflict, important aspects of which are subliminally experienced. Self-management involves apparently hard-to-generalize combinations of perception and reaction. Freud's schema of id-ego-superego attempts to compartmentalize discretely, for example, the internal drives of animalism, self-protection, and conscience as these are represented in the complicated emotional and ratiocinative processes underlying visible behavior. But interpretation of behavior in a Freudian manner or in that of other standard schools of thought may overlook the influence of a highly organized milieu in securing behavioral responses that destroy both the individual's sense of control and his ability to maintain continuity of behavior over time.

As demands upon the individual multiply under the innumerable pressures of modern life, motivations for behavior become the more difficult to define: Freud's tripartite system of causation seems overly simplified. Categories into which internal mechanisms of behavior may be neatly grouped are even less easily defined, for they tend to blur and overlap. The existential view of life gives a more modern explanation in that it asserts nonexplanation. But Existentialism, like

Stoicism in Greek times, serves only a relative handful of individuals as a workable prop to existence. What it has to say to the masses, who might find in its rejection of the intellectualization of behavior the key to their acceptance of counterconditioning, may never be known.

For our schools still force learners, outrightly or by implication essentially in the old direction, toward some kind of explanation after the fact rather than toward effective use of unexplained sources of personal power in adapting to the stream of events. The conventional school wisdom, in short, still holds that rational process constitutes *everyone's* path to learning. This attitude, in environmental times, means short-changing both society and the individual. Indeed, failure to develop reflexive and subliminally effective counterlearning is a blow against the person from which, in the average case, regardless of his talents, he never successfully recovers.

The way to counterlearning lies not in more and better intellectualizing; it lies, for the average man, in counterconditioning, a conditioning that does not overwhelm him with dissonance but keeps him on the path of positive adaptation to a difficult life situation. This will of course be a subtle undertaking, one that can be directed only by a minority able to exert the necessary initiatives and controls (but, hopefully, not an old-style minority, an elite dedicated solely to self-preservation. It will be an undertaking that will subject the "mass individual" to new patterns of stimuli, patterns suited to a wholly new and integrative view of his relationship to society. In some measure these patterns are already bombarding individuals in advanced societies, but their overall direction is very unclear. Sooner or later, their operational form will become as apparent as their principle of operation must now be: In the workings of a market economy, subject always to increasing efforts from above to rationalize every human weakness and turn it to commercial or (as in the case of Marxist societies) governmental advantage, human ability to resist opportunistic or socially destructive impulses depends *on the availability of a counterstimulus,* one that appears at the right time and in the proper degree of psychological strength. Further, society will have to reinforce in some appropriate way the behavior that this counterstimulus brings forth, or the entire process will prove meaningless.

In old-fashioned Victorian societies, with their strong class distinctions and wealth sufficient for all those clever enough and determined enough to force their way into outer edges of the charmed circle of power, the idea of schooling to produce gentlemen presupposed the existence of a permanent uneducated class from which the upper class stood absolutely distinct in level of learning and management of behavior. In contemporary, post-industrial societies the communications revolution has altered this distinction radically. Physical inheritance being no respecter of class distinctions, poor children with the potential for access to the elite level of a technological order are less and less willing to agree to being relegated to the status of second-class citizens. As each generation passes, the urge to make *fair* competition the basis of social progress will dictate that fair competition in formal education also be recognized in the provision and organization of learning opportunity.

This recognition must, in turn, be based on the view of post-industrial life that acknowledges self-development through an optimum education as the primary key to both individual and group adaptation. Practically speaking, in a steadily more crowded environment, there are two important and not entirely mutually exclusive benefits from this concept of education; it will serve a) as a primary means of insuring that society can better withstand the shocks of ever-swifter change, by pointing the individual down the path of self-development and not the path of hyperindividualistic exploitation of others that by now endangers society by its moral and, indeed, even physical destructiveness; b) as an indirect means of enforcing compliant behavior by the individual in his interface with the nonhuman environment, that is, by influencing his patterns of use of nonrenewable resources, habits in respect to disposal of wastes, and so on.

To obtain these benefits from education, great efforts to develop suitable learning approaches must be put forth. I do not for one moment suggest that in this process cultivation of the conscious mind be abandoned. But the conditions and the times suggest a many-sided design for learning by which substantial change might be wrought in that realm of human behavior which is based on unreflected assumptions or established habits affecting the physical and social environment. It would be unrealistic to assume that in this undertaking individuals can achieve the needed capabilities and standards unaided. There will be a need for social reinforcement at every step of the way.

Social Reinforcement and Environmental Behavior

In the environmental context, social reinforcement is the concept that mandates social support for human behavior of an environmentally sound character. In an open, pluralistic society this formula seems, for the present at least, nearly impossible to define in practical terms. However, it appears probable that the changing circumstances of group life over the next several decades will heighten public understanding of basic issues to such an extent that consensus regarding the definition of both environmentally appropriate individual behavior and the modes of reinforcing it by society may be achieved. The steadily increasing public concern over use and abuse of physical resources in North American society, for example, seems to suggest that behavior affecting the physical environment may already be receiving the kind of public scrutiny that would lead to such definition.

In the 1970s the world's advanced societies entered upon a period of shortages in the supply of many consumer goods, not excluding foodstuffs. It would be altogether too easy to dismiss this phenomenon as temporary. A more appropriate interpretation, given present and projected population figures, is that these societies will be forced to enter the field of resource managenent on a steadily increasing scale. In fact, some evidence that this is indeed already happening is not too hard to find.

Consider the field that now has such importance to the entire functioning of a technological society, that of resource recovery. Evident progress has been made in this area. For example, potentially effective recovery techniques for dealing with solid wastes are a reality and implementation on a full scale seems only a matter of time. Yet, given the consistently rising rate of population growth, it would prove a grave mistake to assume that a productive recovery technology alone can overcome the problem of absolute resource limitations. There must also be made available to society, through its system of legal restraints as well as through its informal and educational enforcement structure, equally effective ways and means of curbing excessive use of natural resources. In the long run it would seem likely that extra-legal controls will prove more satisfactory to a sophisticated citizenry than precisely defined legal sanctions. An education effective in securing mass behavior consistent with resource management over considerable periods of time would of necessity be an education that could govern both consciously determined and intuitive behavior in equal measure.

The intersocial aspect of man's environment would, naturally, be subject to the same pressures and trends as that of the management of resources. Social relations are the sum and substance of a social environment just as natural resources and man's relations to them are the essential components of a physical environment. However, in this domain, with its strong element of irrational political undertow, progress seems likely to lag behind that in the area of resource management, where needs and the compulsion for definite remedial action must be felt earlier — for obvious reasons. A dual system of education, nevertheless, balancing conditioned learning with learning for awareness according to individual requirements, can lead to appropriate behavioral results in both domains.

Much of this futurist education will involve providing people with opportunities to substitute other, previously unavailable behavior for that of today. In essence, the struggle to delineate substitute opportunities by which mass society can divert its attention from resource abuse and abuse of others becomes the struggle for ideas. The computer age has opened to a special class of thinkers that view. of the universal flow of events which permits a much more realistic application of theories of multiple-variable, continuum-related cause-effect to human behavior. The central problem in this development is the extreme difficulty of detecting hidden variables that affect outcomes, along with the definition of variables that have a diffuse social base. Systems theory, however, has already brought about greater efficiency in the average large business enterprise by achieving a clearer operating definition of cause-effect elements, and this experience cannot be lost on the host of today's educational planners.

Systems theory as applied in formal education has perhaps tended to produce little more than empty reportage of outcomes that cannot be well measured, are not readily interpretable, have little bearing on any realistic scheme of human values, and (of most immediate significance) relate more to influences outside the range of manipulation of the system managers than they do to manipulable forces within the system. Even so, what work has been done, while it demonstrates the extraordinary complexity of cause and effect in learning, sets a necessary direction. It shows that it will be in society's eventual best interest to pursue policies of shaping formal education systematically, to the ends of adaptation and of making the reinforcement by society of behavior suited to environmental needs a priority even while the complexity of such a task still dazzles anyone who dares to think honestly about it.

Society's ways of reinforcing environmentally appropriate behavior are theoretically unlimited but for practical purposes one must begin the work of change at some point where at least minimum observable effect might be realized. Our attention must turn to the young and, especially where the question of effective conditioning arises, to the school. We take a step toward environmental reality by accepting that conditioning, and the social reinforcement that can make it take proper hold must be provided to the individual *at a suitably impressionable age.* Even while we accept the difficulties of using the school as a counterweight to negative influences on the child from the home and general social environment, we cannot (as even careful theorists like Jencks sometimes seem to imply) write off the school totally as an institution unable to aid the individual in his quest for adaptive capabilities.

"De-schooling" society or the complete bypassing of schools or any formal institutions of education are solutions that will solve fewer problems than they will create. Institutions with a natural social idealism, once destroyed or emasculated through the contempt of the society they were meant to serve, are likely to prove difficult indeed to replace. It has hardly been shown beyond doubt that the school could not, for example, even without wholesale change, provide individuals with reinforcements to behavior of a greater adaptive and survival value. All we can say with some certainty is that society has not viewed the school as an institution worthy of being made the primary organ of social change. Further, society has also shown no willingness to support activism on behalf of radical school reorganization (e.g., by taking seriously such sweeping recommendations for change in higher education as those made by the so-called Newman Committee to the U.S. Department of Health, Education, and Welfare in 1971 [22]).

The dawn of an environmental age calls for not only new priorities but also more flexible social reactions to the need for change. Yet change does not necessarily mean the total destruction of existing institutions or traditions. It more likely means their logical modification in light of graduallly emerging life imperatives. Such seems to be the case with the contemporary school as an institution of social service.

Why should society give up on schools before their complete social possibilities have been explored? Accountability, discovery learning, vouchers, protocol materials — these and the myriad other new practices and approaches designed for grafting upon the present school operation are alike in only one respect, but a very important one: all are intended to be applied to the school as an institutionally *developed* entity, a unit whose evolution within society is complete, upon which no change can be worked that would disturb the relationship already in force between school and society. What is missing is a key by which the interests of society and those of the school can be made more nearly one. Up till now, a stranglehold of tradition and vested interests has kept the school operating within an overly limited framework. Environmental development of the whole society, however, bespeaks a need for positive change that sooner or later neither school nor society will have reason to resist. It is correct to assume that, given the socially integrative thrust of environmental development, the concept of the school as an institution neatly separated from its supporting social milieu will soon enough become only a memory. But what form might the environmental "school of tomorrow" take? This question is worth extended consideration.

School As a Social Enterprise

Learning at any level follows the continuum of human perceptions over time. Its ultimate outcomes in patterns of behavior depend much on the extent to which certain behavioral responses are reinforced over time and others are not. As has been pointed out, society itself possesses a significant potential, not developed as yet with any degree of awareness by the elite of planners, for managing individual reinforcements on a mass social basis.

To explore this issue further in educational perspective, more thought must be given to the individual case. Social reinforcement of learning comes about, apparently, largely as a result of the learner's engaging in enterprises having some individually perceived social importance. Commitment to such engagement, following intake of some suitable learning stimulus, is far more effective in terms of steadiness and continuation of effort when the individual acts from his own conviction of need rather than from social pressure. But where the one leaves off and the other begins remains an open question and the potential significance of social reinforcement is by this very uncertainty underscored. The experimental work and general theory of Skinner and his followers suggest how central to behavior must reinforcement be; environmental social theory could scarcely ignore the possible use on a large scale of behavior reinforcement in the interests of social integration, in any case.

How, then, might all this relate to schooling? What the youthful scholar, particularly the teen-age child, lacks is not willingness to learn or the ability to restrain his own behavioral perversity so much as the sense of school as the valid, ongoing context of a social enterprise that can draw him — even as the latest commercially dictated cultural interests spawned by Madison Avenue and the media now draw him and form his other-oriented life style — into pursuit of engrossing experiences that he can, along with his age-mates, genuinely enjoy and accept. I suggest here a broadly defined plan of a system of schooling, one that could be adopted by some nations or cultures more readily than by others, and which would have to be modified considerably to suit any given set of specific circumstances.

Imagine a school building as not merely a place of physical incarceration for some hundreds of students for six or seven hours a day, one hundred and eighty.days a year. Imagine instead that this building is the headquarters of an enterprise with worldwide communications, production, and marketing interests. The aim of this establishment is not to force a predetermined curriculum upon any student or to insure that certain standardized examinations must be passed at specific chronological points in the student's career. Instead, the aim of this school is to provide an *organizational framework* through which student- and teacher-effort at coping with psychological, social, and economic reality can be funneled. However, as an organization this school differs considerably from the ordinary industrial firm known to adult working society. It maintains only a minimum staff of adult aides to assist and advise in what are essentially student-initiated-and-maintained programs of work; it pursues the profit motive only secondarily; it permits development of multiple individual interests within a loose framework of corporate direction and social consensus.

Teachers in the traditional sense are few in number. Mainly those who are present are persons of considerable experience in nonschool settings, whose areas of relative expertise are many, and whose basic competence is that of the idea-person, one who can suggest and inspire rather than dictate and lecture, one whose imagination and ingenuity make him of far more value to his youthful colleagues than today's typical middle school or high school pedant with his over-glorified and often pedagogically meaningless subject-matter certification. In a single term, the teacher's role in this school is that of *reinforcer-guide.*

Students range in age from about twelve to twenty, combining experimentally the various secondary layers from middle or junior high school through junior college. Grade distinctions are dispensed with, although day-to-day activity and "achievement" logs on individual scholars are maintained by the institution's computers as a matter of course. The learners taken together form a body of workers, a pool of diverse talents; there are investigators, coordinators, planners, theorists, decipherers, translators, technicians, evaluators, analysts, and so on. But specific individual responsibilities are computer-diagnosed and prescribed to take into account inexperience, goal limitations, and other factors relating to the potential efficiency of this particular school as a subsystem within the total social system.

Taking a page from the Marxian book, the internal division

of labor is organized with the help of the computer to avoid the need for excessive individual specialization. There could hardly exist in any case the capability for developing a high degree of specialization among a cross section of youth of this age. Correspondingly, individuals do not continue indefinitely in any one category of work. Categories overlap, and through advance computer organization provision is made for alternation among scholars of all basic performance requirements up to the limits posed by any individual's natural capacity. Yet the computer does not mandate any overall work plan in ignorance of students' wishes. It matches these in all their variety against what it perceives to be the mimimum goals toward which the school as a system must move. Naturally, specification of these goals will be a matter of computer decision-making on the basis of fullest possible information input from all participants in the system. It is probable that by provision of the school's constitution any attempt to disallow the computer's final decision by an executive council or other representative body would be expressly prohibited. Thus the youth of this institution would accept the basic proposition that in learning to adapt for survival and the quintessential social needs of a cybernated society, men will have to accept some decisions based on completeness of information and thoroughness in scanning alternative outcomes as well as a good many decisions still based (as now) on the temporary states of mind of members of small committees or the postprandial digestive condition of an elder of the school board.

This school, then, will manage to operate on only a modest public subsidy, used largely to pay maintenance costs and salaries of the small teacher-consultant staff. Wherever possible, as in the Summerhill model, administrative functions will be carried out by participant teacher-learner groups rather than by administrators brought in from outside. Unlike ordinary business organizations, stress on status divisions and distinctions will be reduced to a minimum and the working principle by which this desideratum might be maintained in

a practical way must be that of continuous rotation of responsibilities among all members of the organization.

Although production of primary industrial products cannot take place in this physically restricted milieu, it is not
impossible to conceive of the school as a legal entity (assuming that state laws were altered to permit such activity)
owning and managing an industrial enterprise located elsewhere. However, since for the foreseeable future such
radical developments will undoubtedly be prevented by the
vested interests of the larger commercial society, the "environmental school" might better give its corporate attention
to less immediately threatening pursuits: information processing and evaluation; internal large- and small-group investigations or studies centering around the proof or disproof
of policy needs or recommendations as put forth by repre-
sentatives of government or business; planning of complex
intellectual and social enterprises within the school organization or similar enterprises undertaken jointly with other
educational institutions of like character (often far removed
geographically and culturally); research and development
activities aimed at developing more precise standards of
external behavior consistent with social living in an environmental age, and ways and means to evoke such behavior with
the least amount of social friction; development of rationales
and practical plans for providing a fairer, more thorough, and
more effective application of social and psychological services
to all members of society.

It will of course quickly be remarked that generations of
"experts" have already wrestled with such problems as these
without achieving significant results. There are two basic
refutations of this objection that must be brought forward
within the context of the "environmental school" here being
developed: a) the overly specialized "expert" not only
represents a particular and specialized point of view, by
definition lacking some aspects of needed generality, but he
also has lost the perspective of indefinite future time along
with his youth and this may be seen as a built-in attitude

automatically prejudicial to consensus; b) youthful idealism, as politicians themselves often concede, has a unique ultimate value in human planning for in its social dimension it seeks to express "what should be" rather than "what is merely possible."

All of what has been thus far described of the "environmental school" has, of course, an aura of relative implausibility without a clearer definition of this institution's relation to the outer society and of the relative independence of the latter shown by the school in its internal organization. This organization, if it merely duplicates today's and yesterday's outworn patterns, will doom the new school as a futurist, model learning enterprise. The assumption that *any* school requires a large caretaker cadre with highly specific and individualized responsibilities, if accepted as an unavoidable requirement, in effect cancels out all hope of change, and especially change in the direction of self-government, which is central to the success of any genuinely environmental social institution.

The complaint that society always has and always will have produced too many teachers and school administrators may be dismissed in this context, not because it fails to state a current social truth but because it does not take into account the extent to which the entire employment structure itself, over all of society, must change radically and swiftly in the course of a few decades of rapid increase in cybernations and rationalizations of social processes. Today's teachers and administrators are already more numerous than circumstances require and sooner or later the "make-work" arrangements that give them positions and job security will yield to more goal-oriented planning approaches that will of necessity concentrate upon fulfilling the learners' needs rather than upon preserving socially irrational and outmoded employment practices.

In short, with the development of a socially self-starting and self-regenerating group motivation among students to participate in a primarily youth-run and youth-benefiting enterprise, watchdog functions will cease to be of significance and will, where they are needed, be carried out by the school community itself with help from computers in the decision-making process. This and other aspects of the "hands-off" self-governance permitted by the larger society will express the latter's reinforcement of new, more adaptive and (in the long run) more effective learning experiences better than any financial largess to the school, or other visible forms of support. Society's only possible excuse for intervention with some "corrective" action would be an obvious and complete degeneration of internal self-government. None of the completely altered relationship between the formal institution of learning and the society it serves could have been envisioned in the past, because the atmosphere of adult social coercion automatically bred a continuous and self-perpetuating suspicion by youth of the adult society's motives. In turn this suspicion resulted in a permanent and ubiquitous resistance to the learning process, no matter what forms that process might take.

It should not be thought that the environmental school of coming days will automatically divorce itself from this difficulty. A trial-and-error period must be anticipated. However, since an essentially caretaker concept of schooling will have been replaced by a concept of learning through social and self-reinforcement, the problem in attaining operational security will be different from what it was in the old system. In any case, the key to such security would lie in comprehensive, advance general planning. This assumption covers a broad scope of possibilities.

Facilities are perhaps of least importance, but if many of the newer school-architectural uses, better suited as they are to a crowded environment, could be employed, certain of the vicious reinforcements to antisocial behavior of students so common in today's urban school settings might be avoided. Even so, it is not impossible that older school plants could, with some modifications, prove adequate to the drastically new learning approach of an environmental school. Again, some room for experimentation without prejudice in early phases of the changever must be assumed.

As the environmental approach to schooling comes more and more into prominence, the "free-school" philosphy will emerge as a leading element in the pragmatic orientation of the new system. Suggestion rather than coercion (admitting to begin with the difficulties this policy may pose) must determine the degree to which learners use both their time and the resources of the school to good purpose. Specific and detailed goal determinations for the students in their work as individual scholars can be supplied only gradually, as cases permit over time. A revised concept of efficiency in learning, constantly related to a known body of facts regarding the individual — facts gathered and continually reevaluated by computers — will center on development of the person in relation to an evolving goal of adaptation rather than to mastery of predigested and sequentially ordered information, which today is an unproved assumption of the effectiveness of standardization of knowledge according to certain experts' perceptions. Individualization of learning, with the aid of high-speed computers to become widely available in the next generation or so, will in this way assume a greater reality and cease to remain merely a catchword in the mouths of verbally progressive school administrators.

This individualization, effective in the degree to which it satisfies the individual student that he is performing a socially appropriate function, cannot be a one-way proposition; it must be given social reinforcement, which will take different shapes depending on circumstances. If it occurs in sufficient measure through normal interpersonal contact in the average situation, this will meet any reasonable expectations. The artificial buildup of personality cults and hero worship cannot come to exist internally in this institution; all those concerned with the learning process will have enough difficulties for the indefinite future in fending off such inanities bearing down on them in various cybernated forms from the larger outer society. Ubiquity, availability, and attractive arrangement in space and time of learning stimuli within the school may also be depended upon to offer further inducement to self-development to those students not motivated through social encouragement to develop their own directions of inquiry. A small group of unmotivated or marginally motivated youth must naturally be given special assistance by counseling personnel or other suitable functionaries.

One may well pose the question: What of subject matter in all this broad-scale planning? The answer, in broadest terms, is that only such subject matter will be made available for learning as is appropriate to the learner's present requirements and as will (indicated via computer analyses) aid in maintaining his motivation for continued learning. Ongoing projects, individual and group, numbering in the hundreds and thousands even for a single school, will instead constitute the core "learning subjects." These will cover almost every conceivable possibility within the spectrum of intellectual and personal development, ranging from archaeological expeditions in preparation and execution with the aid of experienced professionals, through development of an exchange of videotaped programs by which American students demonstrate usages in their language to French counterparts (and vice-versa), to preparing an instructional film on hydroponic gardening or mitosis or garbage collection or fashions around the world. The possibilities are endless, and they are not limited to what the few adult experts present can recommend; they involve input and selection of ideas from all concerned in the learning process, with assistance from ever-available computers. They necessarily presume a structure of experience and activity that will require, no matter how individualized any student's path of development, an acquaintance at some point along the continuum of learning with those basic capabilities (e.g., skills involved in "learning how to learn") needed for maximum potential adaptation by the individual to the society of tomorrow.

One other question arises logically at this point: How does a degree of apparent order come to exist in all this expenditure of energy and how can one after all guarantee that every student's line of growth has the socially and individually valid basis that has been assumed? In part, the answer to such a question must state that in allowing freedom for growth one must also permit freedom to experiment. Youth's inherent right to experiment, when it runs hard against society's imperatives of control, can only be mitigated or turned aside in some degree; it cannot be destroyed. Society must therefore itself render adaptive judgments based on a margin-for-error theory and an assumption of which among opposite value outcomes constitutes the greater and which the lesser evil. In the future society as it has in fact been envisioned by many social philosophers of today, change and flexibility will be the canons of life and our contemporary passion for security at any cost will seem like a distant dream. Man's progress toward the ideal of environmental balance requires a more tenable balance between experiment and tradition, between needed newness and the valuable remnants of an older order. If the school is indeed the spearhead of tomorrow, its right to experiment must be socially validated.

Yet there is a far more practical and immediately appropriate partial answer to the question of order amid growth; it relates to the educational uses of that still underrated, unique piece of modern machinery — the computer. People everywhere complain of what they see as a devastating combination of forces already arrayed against them: government, business, a mass society, *and* the computer. But reduced to a basic premise, this complaint merely consists in a rejection in the name of sacred individualism of *anyone's* right to invade private life and (worse still) to do so systematically. In this point of view one sees the tremendous residual strength of the tradition that in its most pedestrian evocation states that "you mind your business and I mind mine." The increasing inapplicability of this defensive and morally evasive definition of private rights to the needs of an environmentalized society has been recognized by the younger generation in its ineffectual but not easily forgotten struggles against the "Establishment" all over the Western world during the post-World War II decades. In the society to come, those with "something to hide" will find themselves placed ever more firmly under the scrutiny of an "open-information" system. To the extent that such a system is designed to further public, as against private, ends, it will naturally favor those who (like the young) have nothing to hide. In America of the 1970s this "open-information" system has already in some part entered the operative stage: the Watergate case, for example, shows how impossible it is for even the most powerful and clandestinely functioning branch of the American government to veil indefinitely from public knowledge information of real significance to society as a whole.

It is thus a new social attitude toward information and its uses, as well as a vastly more efficient information system (with the computer at its core), that the school of tomorrow inherits. Computer science and systems theory necessarily have brought society into a much more regularized relationship with the organizational principle. Society, however unrecognizable the phenomenon may be to the casual observer, is becoming steadily more *organized,* and this means that the individual to exist in such a society must in turn bend increasingly to a self-discipline that mirrors the sterner social discipline emerging around him.

Surface reflection at this point seems to suggest that today's youth in advanced societies are daily becoming less and less capable of developing such self-discipline. But this observation reveals a lack of appreciation for the social-psychological basis of youthful behavior. To this point in history no society has existed that did not rely on dictation from above, from the established adult community, in systematizing educational practice. Indeed, a survey of the educational history of the last several centuries would reveal that the process of ordering education first and foremost to suit adult society's (rather than the learner's) needs has gradually become the dominant *modus operandi* in every

national education system. It is one of the great ironies of
modern times that the arrival of the advanced technology
that would allow so inflexible a process to be established
beyond the power of anyone to change also has presented
society with its single best hope for making learning a socially
and individually meaningful experience — through the
systematizing capability of computer technology.

Youth are often quoted to the effect that they are violently
opposed to being "programmed from birth to death," as modern cybernated society seems to them to require. But this is
not the same as saying that they refuse to accept the need
for programming of the individual in the interests of minimum maintenance of a complex, fragile society *when the
individual himself can participate meaningfully in the process.* This difference is significant and worth pondering. It
suggests that systematization of external life is not the issue;
rather, it is a matter of who does the systematizing, with
what intent, and with what results for *particular* individuals
and for society as a whole.

The contemporary school constitutes a perfect example of
a social institution regulated and systematized in its functioning entirely from above. Some seven-odd decades ago Dewey,
in *Democracy and Education,*[23] established the classic case
for systematization *from below,* but an unstable, repressive
society has found it expedient to ignore that embarrassing,
radical statement of belief. Thus, while the incessant clamor
for school reform goes on, this essential underlying problem
remains unresolved. Meantime, without direction in its value
component, educational practice merges imperceptibly but
irreversibly with technological development. The computer
stands as both symbol and primary working tool of this
marriage between man the learner and man the system-
maker. In an age of fast-arriving environmental imperatives,
new generations must have an optimum opportunity to use
mechanical adjuncts in the process of adaptive learning.
How, in broad outline, might this be accomplished?

One Possibility: Computer Assistance in
the Search for a New, More Credible Learning

Despite claims to the contrary, computers in educational usage have barely entered the post-infancy stage. What work has been done to date is concerned mainly with applying principles of programming to some fixed body of predetermined, specialized subject matter, or it has had to do with the improvement of typical administrative practice in dealing with such vexing day-to-day problems as record keeping, class scheduling, and cost analysis. It has not yet been applied in any concerted and continuous way to the much more demanding and educationally substantive problems of creating and maintaining a structure of learning suited to the diverse requirements of those who will live in a highly cybernated future world of vast complexity and swift, unrelenting change. This next step can be delayed for a time by social obtuseness and resistance to experiment; it cannot be held off indefinitely.

Chief among the computer's more advanced educational uses will be as the major aid in individualization of instruction and of curricula. It is the only tool capable of providing carefully designed, comprehensive learning progressions that can be corrected or redirected as they are underway. That is, it can broaden or deepen, allow greater freedom or create greater restraint as needed in the interest of continuous student progress. It can and will also aid in the interlocking of concerns of groups of individual students at certain points of curricular commonality. It will become the prime tool of individual and group diagnosis and planning, the tool for continuous monitoring of outcomes, and the instrument through which follow-up and evaluation can best be maintained. But none of this, in the present state of computer science, will happen automatically. Men must apply thought to the use of computers in education. A period of experimentation, as well as of sheer trial and error, lies in the immediate future.

One crucial problem that can be resolved only by the assistance of the computer is that of maintaining for each individual, through a series of stages in time a suitable range of learning choices. The input of data required to achieve this goal must necessarily reach a volume scarcely comprehensible to a nonmathematician. A development of this kind, if it is to occur, assumes continuing breakthroughs in the building of computers able to "think for themselves," machines that can generate the kind of total knowledge of an individual so that a genuinely apppropriate stimulus can be fed him at any specific time: an individualized stimulus, one almost impossible to define given current linguistic and conceptual limitations. But generations will pass before such a capability is reached, or before the public accepts a need to place such confidence in a mere machine. Meanwhile, interim expansion of human service professions (e.g., guidance, psychiatry) must serve to take up to the extent possible a dangerous and increasing slack in the young person's motivation to learn. This is made all the more difficult by the strong resistance to substantive experimentation on the part of the governing sector (i.e., trustees, administrations, teachers, unions) in mass education.

Another problem with which the computer must become involved is that of analysing and aiding the social reinforcement process, especially in prescribing sanely for cases of malingering, ennui, discontinuity, retreat from the learning stance, or general mental fatigue. The average classroom teacher has long ago played his last trump cards in fighting this battle, and he can hardly be expected to achieve any further success until a drastic alteration of the learning milieu has taken place. Since no one, under the ground rules of democratic life, can be forced to act — in theory — against his own will, this work of altering the learning environment to develop maximum social reinforcement must of course be pursued with forbearance.

Use of the computer in dealing with this aspect of learning management is thus naturally fraught with dangers and one hardly need be surprised that it has not yet been explored in any realistic sense. In part this is the case because behavioral scientists are as yet still too preoccupied with discussing philosophies or principles of behavior to take up seriously questions relating to the systematic direction of behavior. But certain deep-seated social fears are also involved: a) that essential rights of privacy could be all too easily infringed; b) that the human dimension symbolized by the teacher-pupil or therapist-patient relationship will be upset so that a breakdown of the expert's status in society will naturally follow (in effect the man-man interface of the classroom, the guidance office, the psychiatrist's sanctum, etc., is replaced by a man-machine interface).

The second of these fears has a basis in reality, to be sure, but only to the extent that as time passes it is in the social interest to eliminate from society's payroll those "experts" who do not in fact serve a useful purpose (e.g., many school-teachers without a contribution to make to the learning process because of their narrow specialization, unimaginativeness, etc.), separating these unneeded people from those whose services are indispensable. Anyone familiar with American teacher education over the last two decades will be aware that in a general way society has been demanding and to some degree getting a more rationalized ordering of human resources for the public schools, even though the process of separating teachers who genuinely contribute from those who merely put in time has barely gotten underway. That this process will continue and produce some perhaps at present unanticipated turns over succeeding decades may be assumed.

The issue of infringing private rights was earlier referred to in connection with the question of new social attitudes toward information and the advent of an open-information system. It seems likely that the whole existing concept of privacy will, in light of rapid and qualitative changes in man's physical and social environment, require comprehensive reexamination in coming decades. There may be required alterations in legal codes and public attitudes to conform to changed conditions of group life. Current interpretations of various laws of privilege, such as private property rights, rights of access, and the like, may shift so as to mirror more properly new areas of social need. Protection of personal possessions and perquisites that are legitimate to proper functioning of society must of course continue. But social evolution is necessarily tied to a new standard of information processing; this standard is inescapably implicit in the whole trend of educational practice geared to futurism and adaptation and symbolized in the computer.

Because today's youth are educated in a system deluged in the flow of free information, therefore, they will acquire and are acquiring greater flexibility of attitudes and an expanded sense of social purpose. The adult-designated *antisocial* behavior of college youth in the decade of the 1960s may indeed have been antisocial in the context of those times. But in futurist context such behavior was a demonstration that the secret agreements and Machiavellian cabals by which the American political system is run and economic spoils distributed are too profitless for succeeding generations to pursue. It is not the present generation but the future generations that will bear the burden of dismantling the old structure of inequitably shared power. Hidden government and all the other evils of today and yesterday are bound to become victims of the new information technology. If youth did not have a positive interest in building a future society more open and unrepressive, it would not have any interest in the development of open-information systems. But the two are inseparable; to have one, youth must have the other. This need outweighs any social fear for the individual's private life and mandates the use of technology as a backup to existing systems of social reinforcement for learning. This is only logical and reasonable, for by means of his "new" education the man of tomorrow will be better enabled to adjust to the demands of social life, a life substantially different from that of his forebears in its progressive deemphasis of power seeking for ego gratification, exploitation of others and of the physical environment, and aggressive behavior generally. It will have instead progressive emphasis on a balance of tissue and creature needs with self-fulfillment needs, mental and moral search as the basis of intellectual life, and social service as the basis of group life.

I have discussed at some length and in highly general terms how the computer can assist in this venture to provide a "new" education. A few remarks are also apropos regarding organizational principles and pedagogical assumptions on which this effort will be based. The overall operating plan has earlier been mentioned and somewhat elaborated. In practical terms, social reinforcement of learning must translate into innumerable individual acts of encouragement — by older students of younger ones, or vice-versa, by adjunct personnel of students, by student groups of individuals and of other groups, and so on. This will be possible to the extent that the school exists as an independent, self-sustaining unit and not as a mere creature of controlling interest in the larger society. The more the school can be made to function independently, like a business or governmental entity with an economic or investigatory or creative purpose, the more likely it will be to maintain itself and develop internally as a viable institution. This will not be easy to achieve, for it contravenes the age-old view that a school is merely an exercise ground for neophytes and not an integral, evolving, functional unit of society.

While the principle of social reinforcement covers motivational considerations in this "school of tomorrow," no pedagogic principle will have more importance than that of direction of interest. If the goals of learning in this school were, as in the more traditional setting, primarily academic, exalting objective knowledge as an end in itself without reference to immediate and near-future uses of such knowledge, today's increasing difficulties in maintaining both student interest in and student application to learning activities would of course continue. But by maximizing social sources of motivation and dovetailing these with plans of instruction

designed, with extensive computer assistance, to engage the
youthful mind with utmost continuing personal appeal, the
environmental school will presumably serve the purpose of
doing what no school has to this point in history been able
to do — promote learning during the formal experience of
education and promote it successfully. In essence, students
will be seeking knowledge because they must have it to serve
present as well as future purposes. This is the hallmark of
adaptive learning and in conformity with man's environmental needs.

It will perhaps be complained that the system here described in such broad terms is nevertheless unworkable because it relates to no specific criterion of ultimate performance, that is, it does not program the individual to attain
certain competencies needed to perform adequately in specialized employment following his schooling. In answer to this
pragmatic objection, some counterclaims must be pointed
out. While the student of this institution has not studied a
particular subject matter in the old way, he has been involved
in a far less academic and far more practical application of
certain elements of knowledge than would have been possible
under the traditional approach. And this could well provide
him with a better, rather than a poorer, job-relevant education. Further, in countering the objection that his "training"
has been insufficiently related to a specific future occupation, there should be pointed out the far more desirable
motivation that this student will carry with him from the
school into the world of work as well as an ability to "learn
how to learn" developed out of necessity in the environmental school, with its context of maximum social reinforcement. In addition to all this, one must keep in mind certain
conditions in the outer society very likely to obtain at the
indefinite point in the future here under consideration:
a) the system of graduate professional education will continue to evolve along its present lines of direction, so that a
further buildup in specific, specialized entrance requirements
may be expected, and in some manner the environmental

school must prepare its students to meet such requirements; b) the nature of work in industry over the indefinite future will be such that more ample on-the-job education will be provided and in this situation the background of the graduate of an environmental school, with its task-oriented approach to learning, should provide both himself and his employer many natural advantages; c) the system of student evaluation will have been significantly improved and knowledge of the capabilities of graduates will be vastly expanded; in the environmental school there may well be, for example, not only continuous computer monitoring of student progress but also school-leaving and other examinations generated by the computer, thoroughly individualized and based on integration (at the student's expected level of capability) of his own complete and unique learning experiences in this school from his twelfth to his twentieth year.

A significant feature of all progress in these directions, it must be pointed out again, will be the acceptance of mechanical assistance in all phases of the process of engineered learning. Variety in experiences and maximum curricular balance for the individual student, consistent with his mental potential and incipient interests as well as his probable life circumstances, must be guaranteed. Only the immense scanning power of the computer can make this guarantee a reality. Today's computers, probably even the ILLIAC IV, capable of performing a billion operations per second,[24] are still inadequate to the incredible demands of the tasks that must be carried out. But technology is eventually equal to the challenge, provided that man can accept the results of these developments in terms of change in his own behavior. Adequate machines will be constructed; men will need to make use of them to further the end of environmental adaptation, or indeed, as many critics have warned, he will be abused by them. The place in which to begin, accepting the full range of risk entailed, is where behavior itself begins: the sphere of learning.

Foremost among the developer's problems will be that of

designing forms of computer assistance to learning that permit person and computer to work as partners, not as a system of leader and follower in which a man is dominated body and soul by a machine so clever that he becomes psychologically a total dependent. In addition, there exists the possibility that computers of such competence will come into being that a machine will literally be able to scan sample future behavior patterns of society and individuals, match them with accurately projected future levels of physical and social resource availability, and create a relatively complete advance picture of all major decision-points any single individual with a given set of characteristics may expect to meet in his lifetime. In other words, computers can theoretically be programmed to preconsider accurately the substantive events of both group and individual life into even the fairly distant future. Merely the supposition that such a capability could be brought into existence has significance for educational policy. The likelihood, however remote at present, that the uncertainty of fate might no longer shadow a young person's expectations as it has through all the past ages of man raises for formal education fundamental questions of purpose and direction.

To the person without intellectual incentive, as well as for the society in which he lives, this potential extension of control over individual and social behavior through technology may prove a nightmare of pointless suffering and struggle. For society it poses with the typical steady and increasing pressure of the cybernation principle a gradually intensifying battle between the forces that hold a working social structure together and those which would tear it apart. For the individual lacking the capacity for self-development, it unquestionably signifies a closing off, one by one, of those paths of uncontrolled behavior which formerly with a sufficient degree of social sanction allowed him to maintain his necessary ego strength and sense of justification by exploiting elements of his immediate environment. Given a stopping of this exploitation by society's fiat, what can be done to preserve social order and keep the individual sane?

The overly theoretical, easier assumption that a uniformly better humanity must be bred, and as swiftly as possible, to permit society its best chance of survival in this period of radical change has been considered at length earlier in this chapter. The same arguments hold. Genetic engineering may or may not provide a way out of the dilemma faced by advanced societies as they enter the age of total cybernation. Nurture of potentials for more adaptive behavior remains the more reasonable and pragmatic approach for the present and intermediate future. But the kind of nurture to be provided must be determined carefully.

Here again, the basic environmental premise of the absolute priority of self-development in a social context of third-stage human evolution seems to provide a considerable part of the answer to this otherwise crushing problem. And in marking off this priority, in turning humanity in upon its own resources literally and figuratively, it is of importance to concede both man's long-range capabilities and his permanent inadequacies. The computer, while it still depends on man for initial programming, possesses a theoretical capacity to outthink man. As computer science develops, the "stupidity" that may correctly be attributed to previous and present generations of these machines seems likely to become a thing of the past. Our technology can already produce machines that evaluate their own performance according to given criteria and then go on to "improve" initial criteria without the human programmer knowing why such shifts in criteria values have occurred.[25] Serious scientists "do not think it at all unlikely that someday computers, supplied with feelings and even moral values, will make decisions based on those feelings and values, as well as on what their sensors perceive."[26]

Man does not have to view himself as a competitor of this invention of his. If he does, he will have entered a race he cannot win. He would do better to see himself as a creature of residual passions and irrationalities, one who can seek the aid of machines in controlling the life around him but who must finally depend on his own inner resources as the basis of meaningful existence. He should be reminded of what he possesses that the computer does not: the power of absolute involvement on an emotional plane; his ability to dream and deceive himself as to the "inevitable" meaninglessness of life; his capacity for self-development through progressive elaboration of his affective, aesthetic, and spiritual interests.

Today's adult generations are already making their difficult adjustments, albeit largely without their own notice, to the web of cybernations that gradually and inexorably has come into being to enforce the behavioral mandates of the first post-industrial decades. Because tomorrow's adult generations will be involved in merging this cybernation with the even deeper-lying cybernation of a coming environmental age, the difficulties of adjustment and adaptation will be greater in the decades just ahead. Learning to cope and to grow will have become, as the twentieth century fades and the twenty-first looms so much larger on the horizon, more than ever the prime challenges of social life.

Today's schools cannot provide a suitable preparation for the citizen of the future, given their limitations. They are out of tune with contemporary needs and their policy setters have not yet begun to consider the needs of an even more demanding future. What has been described as "the environmental school of the future" is one attempt to provide an institutional framework for meeting some of those needs more realistically.

7

Afterword — The Realities of Modern Life and a Workable Philosophy of Environmental Education

An educational philosophy for an age of adaptive behavior cannot be formed in a vacuum, remote from the conditions of social life. It must recognize those conditions and establish from them and from past experience generalizations suitable for use in present and future decision-making. There are two broadly defined and inter-related conditions of organized life in industrial societies that are of governing importance in any philosophic consideration of the direction of educational effort in our contemporary world: the cybernated social environment, and man's increasing dependence on energy resources as the key factor limiting or controlling the development of civilization along the paths hitherto followed. Both of these elements require more than passing attention in the present context.

Cybernetics is defined as a science that optimizes control over essential functions of the nervous system and brain by the systematization of communications input. It involves a comprehensive management of basic data and feedback, and

191

the progressive assertion of those mechanisms of control which are in the systematizer's interest to develop. It provides the model case for use in all, or nearly all, decision-making situations. I use the terminology of this science in its broadest possible significance. "Essentially, cybernetics deals with the dynamics of an entire system, including its sub-systems and the controls which limit or affect the functions of that system". [1]

Man as an individual is the point of intersection of a plethora of overlaps in cybernation, or at the mercy of impulses aimed at maximizing interests of social and economic institutions increasingly given over to management of exploitative stimuli in a consumer society. Feedback to centers of corporate or government control, as it increases in amount and accuracy, permits a more rationalized ordering of the controlling unit's effort as operations continue. The inherent tendency of such a mode of operation is to make more subtle and irresistible the various pressures directed upon the human beings who, in their reactions, determine the success or nonsuccess of the institution concerned. This, in turn, requires ever more careful decision-making within the center of corporate control.

The formal and limited application of principles of cybernetics to educational systems is proceeding in various forms, in particular the "accountability" approach. In these efforts educators encounter basic philosophic and semantic problems which, as they are pragmatically resolved, may determine the effective future limits upon what formal schooling can contribute to social integration in light of environmental requirements. But the issue here is that of how a *totality* of systems affects human behavior; it is the question of what *kind of man* one sees as emerging from the process of comprehensive socioeconomic cybernation. To evolve a philosophy of education for an era of total systematization, one can stipulate an idealized independence toward which to educate, or one can assess the enormous potential for control of human behavior implied in the cybernetics principle and educate for total adaptation to a managed environment. These are the extremes and, as is often the case, real outcomes are likely to fall between such extremes; a socially valid philosophy of education, too, should avoid the incorporation of intransigent and extremist points of view if it is to maintain a foothold in reality.

It would be appropriate to begin by suggesting what can be *done without* in this process. One factor that may be summarily dismissed is the jejune assumption that a philosophy that has a steady reference to concrete reality can espouse any line of policy that is without social and psychological costs. In a society of total interdependence, no undertakings in the social domain are without costs. The treasured Western concept of personal freedom provides the by now most obvious example of this dictum in practice.

The atavistic liberal view of human freedom as a unique constant in a society subject to many-faceted cybernation needs reexamination. Also in need of reexamination is the corollary supposition that constraints upon the freedom of action of individuals, institutions, business enterprises, and government bureaus, operating within a society made up of interlocking cybernated systems, can be reduced without creating additional constraints elsewhere. This is tantamount to saying that it is in the best interests of society as a whole to spread costs equitably throughout the body social. Such a point of view not only fits conceptually the framework of environmental thought; it also implies eventual legal or other practically effective means by which society will, in the interests of all its members, regulate the flow and psychological content of all cybernations.

One other assumption that a contemporary and realistic philosophy of environmental education can do without is that which accepts the inevitability of a continued marriage between cybernetics and the high-consumption culture. Population pressures against dwindling resource supplies will in the decades of the 1980s and 1990s alone drastically reduce the meaningfulness of this marriage. It should not be necessary at this stage of world social development to pass off the fulminations of a Fidel Castro or a Dr. Allende against the principle of a consumer society as just so much Communist crankiness. The growing concern even in such an openly exploitative economy as that of late-twentieth-century U.S.A. for equitable sharing of resources bears out the degree to which the doctrine of "plenty for all" rests on increasingly indefensible assumptions.

Cybernetics therefore begins to assume more and more the look of a forced partner, made to join in the exploitation of physical resources and human behavior potentials in the cause of rankly retrograde over-consumption. An unfavorable population growth rate combined with diminution of resources means increasing human competition for goods, services, and any combination of the two that will enhance experiences satisfying to the individual. Since as time goes on fewer and fewer people would be able to attain these benefits under today's rules of play, the cybernated system that tends to restrict sharing along more equitable lines must become gradually more suspect. To the degree that an ever-higher level of consumption as a working social credo operates in contradiction to social goals that are environmental, it must eventually disappear, and along with it the particular application of the cybernetics principle that aided its remarkably swift, although temporary, rise to dominance in the second half of the twentieth century.

Cybernetics, however, will by no means itself disappear, if only for its potential value in the redirection of human energies toward the sane use of man's sole remaining field of as-yet-unexploited resources — those internal to the individual. A society cybernated into rank high-consumption behavior can also be cybernated in the opposite direction. Once the guiding principle of profit maximization (or in the case of Communist states, of total control by government of the supply-demand function) has been reinterpreted in light of the needs of an environmentally balanced social order, the tools of communications control and mass persuasion can be used to ease man's way to achievement of a more suitable ethic of competition and distribution.

Expressed in this summary fashion, the process of social evolution away from the high-consumption culture is made to sound inevitable and even easy. This would understate the difficulty of the coming reorientation in mass habits. Impulse behavior and the cult of sensory satisfactions before all else in life have never before been the province of so many people who are, at the same time, so poorly equipped in moral and mental powers to resist ungrudgingly the slowly arriving turnaround in mass values. Roughly a billion people in the advanced societies are caught up in the radical high-consumption way of living. Their mode of life is sought after by a majority of the other three billion inhabitants of the planet. There is nothing in the experience of the past to parallel this situation. How can one plan to bring humanity into line with the coming reality that it must unquestionably face?

One must begin with the current situation. The elitism that has long characterized society in all the Western democracies is fading, however gradually. The first, incomplete phase of the process of cybernating society has therefore also begun to pass and, following the logic of social development toward an environmental world order, a new populism has arrived. For the present this populism has merely taken the form of a wider public for the distribution of goods and services, a democratization of consumption that ignores the long-term mismatch between supply and demand. Except for the small vanguard of aware political activists (e.g., Common Cause), there are few evidences of mass comprehension of the absolute need for future democratization on an environmental scale — not only in politics but in the area of production, distribution, and consumption of durable goods and foodstuffs, the area of waste management, and, most important, the area of social cybernetics (the use of communications policy and control for the forwarding of *human* as opposed to purely exploitative purposes).

For the present our attention is relatively fixed upon the negative facets of a consumer culture that seems, literally, to be sweeping the earth. A better life for all is proclaimed not only by the comfortably situated leaders of rich Western democracies, but by tyrant generals who govern small Asian or African states (seldom heard of save in time of war or famine), and even by guerrilla chiefs in the most remote jungle hinterlands. The more advanced Western peoples have in the main set a dangerous example. Futher, they have not as yet summoned the moral strength to resist the waste and degeneracy that first-phase cybernation has imposed. Yet, with every passing generation, constantly better served by information services whose only natural goal must be the promotion of ubiquitous, shared knowledge, cybernetics policy can take new directions. Cybernetics in the environmental age should have the capability of opening up society to immanent, qualitatively superior forms of group living.

It is momentarily comforting but over the long run fruitless to suppose that progress of this kind will come about more or less automatically. In fact, it depends on increased rather than decreased social planning. Deliberate management of social and cultural processes and their direction toward socially objective goals are part of the very nature of environmental change. Planners who are administrators in the widest and least pejorative sense will, as the scope of such change widens, largely replace formally elected politicians as the makers of substantive policy, will be the "idea men" with enough breadth of vision to integrate the myriad elements of the new social system.

The range of such planning will inevitably be greater than any heretofore known. In an ever more crowded world enlightened management must be directed into fields where formerly little or no interference was expected, for example, sensitive consumer fields where in the past a course of wholly free-market enterprise seemed quite sufficient. (The vacillations of the Nixon government in alternately applying controls to and then withdrawing them from the American economy in the late 1960s and early 1970s indicate the problems of an administration that can only manipulate short-term outcomes, and these only relatively well, when it is long-term policy that requires attention. Such a situation re-

flects the essential complexity of an advanced economy, so
that even a conservative administration is forced as a matter
of survival to tamper, however unwillingly and "temporarily"
with what it still regards as the sacred freedoms of the capitalist marketplace.)

Culture, like politics and economics, can itself be expected
to evolve to new states of social relevance. Again, this will be
in part a natural process but in considerable degree it must
also be anticipated and managed. Management of behavior is
not only a likelihood for the future; it is a social and environmental necessity, and it will come. In a sense it is already
here, since pragmatic constraints of many kinds imposed by
government and corporate enterprise in the interests of maintaining a society undisturbed by culturally generated seditions
have already been internalized by an unaware populace. To
savor the probity of this assertion, one should ponder the
degree to which basic individual freedoms "guaranteed" by
the U.S. Constitution are still fully current in late-twentieth-
century North America.

A confusion of ends and means continues that for the
present balks cultural and social progress into the next phase
of man's environmental development, and the high-consumption culture is the cause. It is correct to assume that, as
momentum for change increases, this culture must begin to
decline, with management of behavior gradually taking its
place as the guiding principle of sociocultural development.
But the meliorative character of this alteration in direction
must be seen along with its less desirable features. Management of behavior, through cybernetics, will not appear as
some entirely new phenomenon. What will have taken place,
instead, is the divorce of cybernetics and an over-consumption mania, and the use of management to control behavior
will, in this new world of tomorrow, unquestionably be a
sign of more environmentally and socially appropriate aims.

The distinction is perhaps more readily understood if one
can conceive of the management of human behavior as going
forward on two planes: in the first case, as at present, mass

humanity is manipulated physically and emotionally within a structure of imperatives unrecognized by those whose behavior is directed; in the second case, as in the future, environmentalized social order, mass behavior will undergo direction fully as much as at present but this direction will be far more widely understood and accepted as necessary for the preservation of basic social order and the attainment of social goals. At the same time the better-educated masses will have made needed adjustments to a system of cybernation that turns people steadily and firmly away from actions of pure impulse and inward upon their own self-sustaining, creative resources. In effect, such second-stage management will be environmentally suitable because it will no longer be based on profit and social-class motives but instead will encompass larger goals of social and individual betterment. It will have the specific goal of programming people out of the focus of the old, lower-order management (a policing and coercive operation, basically) and into the higher-level status in which self-development can become a reality for more than a handful of human beings.

As our current high-consumption culture, pushed aside by the harsh imperatives of post-industrial life, gradually fades from the mass consciousness, the only available substitute ethos will with equal deliberateness emerge. Already a class of people — not Maslow's one percent of society that has achieved self-actualization, but a less obvious, less brilliant and numerically more significant group — has attained a level of self-development consistent with the demands of an environmentally functional society. This relative success, an adaptive performance predictive of the less-than-near future, has a basis in *knowledge*. The significant point about such an achievement is not so much that will power, patience, or antisocial bias were involved. The really telling point is that individuals could use knowledge, even that not categorizable academically, as a foil to total management by others, while at the same time not losing a realistic orientation to the transitional society they inhabit.

Drucker stresses the important additional point that the expansion of modern industrial societies has been into the "knowledge" domain as a *whole* rather than into "science" or "technology" per se.[2] Interrelational, general, adaptive, rather than specialized, discrete learning, therefore, is invading the social psyche. This development within the social organism itself dove-tails with the inevitable direction of behavior as man the individual is made to face up ever more frankly to the verities of social life in the environmental future. Unfortunately, none of this works to shift the life priorities of the average man of today. For workers, these gradual changes have come to mean little as yet, because the changes do not now affect substantively the *directed* character of the common man's existence.

If anything, a buildup of first-phase cybernation has narrowed for the present the range of significant choices available to the industrial rank and file. This is in part a result of the exceptionally concentrated profit-maximization techniques utilized to expand markets among the mass of uncritical consumers, something made more readily possible with the increased availability of money for marketing development in the larger, more diversified corporations of today. Further, the compulsion to manage, direct, and exploit should not be seen as limited to industry and its advertising appendages alone: where industry leaves off directing the workingman's volatile behavior into ever more strictly circumscribed avenues of activity, the organized labor movement, the mass media, and various leisure-time industries (e.g., professional spectator sports) take over to do more of the same.

Thus, the "opportunity structure" that would permit a wider diffusion of knowledge worth sharing and using in the self-development process does not exist for practical purposes. This is not to say that the common man must acquire *academic* knowledge in order to reach optimum self-development; his own natural curiosity and desire for more than animal stimulation even now lead him to acquire a more appropriate fund of knowledge for environmental purposes. Rather, the problem is and for some time will remain the *directed* character of his existence: he is too fully enveloped in marketplace cybernation, even, and especially, in his leisure occupations, to move beyond the consumer stereotype.

In summary, current conceptions of freedom and one's "right" to consume as being natural and cost-free components of an advanced society have in no way been brought into line with the realities of a coming age of shortages, excessive human propinquity, and increased control over the individual in his physical and emotional life. The remarkable "knowledge explosion" of the last half of the twentieth century has not yet made its effects felt in the alteration of man's psychic existence and there are strong forces at work to limit the use of the knowlege industry and the cybernetic systems created by that industry to manipulation of mass humanity for fairly narrow ends.   Society as a whole remains less than convinced of the increasing need for planning and management in these next several decades of social evolution. While the popularly conceived role of education in the process of social enlightenment has become awesome and probably impossible, there are in addition serious questions that arise concerning a philosophy of education suitable to a pluralistic society. There is also the question of how workable *any* philosophy, even one acceptable to all on the theoretical level, will prove in practice.

An essential characteristic of the adaptive person of today and tomorrow must be his ability to maintain himself in the rationalized socioeconomic order and at the same time to grow in his inner life. Much of this potential for growth on which the individual depends is necessarily focused on the use of knowledge of a kind not easily susceptible to group-rationalization processes. Strong voices, such as those of Kerr and Brzezinski, argue that the latter knowledge has constantly less relevance to tomorrow, that it is historically irrelevant. Yet college students, the vanguard of tomorrow's adaptives, continue to major in art or history or philosophy and subsequently enter the working world at a permanent disadvantage. They follow overwhelming, immediate interests and attractive personalities in these fields, not the knowledge of their subjects alone. But they do more than this: they blend present interests with an *open* view of the future, a view that recognizes the dangers of tomorrow at the same time that it refuses to close off tomorrow's options. They are preparing for second-stage cybernation, rather than allowing themselves to become fixated on the first stage, with its compulsions to self-protection above all else. If this concept has validity, then there must also be validity in any education that, with an eye to the future, encourages youth to pursue the arts or literature or any exercise of individual imagination that aids the self in moving intellectually beyond the here-and-now of a physically and emotionally stereotyped existence.

If this point of view has pertinence for the individual, it has equal relevance for those concerned with educational management. It presents the first great challenge of an age of environmental individualism to a corps of administrators too many of whom have not yet emerged from the point of view of a management process akin to that of old-line capitalism, the economy-of-scale, assembly-line system. When we look at developments of the last few decades in public education, we are aware of change in progress but we are also aware of the limitations of the context in which such change is taking place:

> since the underlying function of the school system is not challenged by the educational reformers, the only thing that can be done to make it more democratic is to eliminate the barriers facing the "brighter," or more ambitious, children of minority or low-income parents. The attempt has been made over the last several decades, and especially in the 1960's, to apply the principle of merit as fairly as possible (given the class purpose of public education) so that an occupational élite can be chosen from all groups in American society while class and social stratification remains intact. Equality in education will require the elimination of the meritocratic structure, but that reform cannot take place in an educational system whose

purpose is to socialize children into a stratified class society."[3]

Thus the managers of formal education face a double difficulty: a fixed curriculum that militates against the acquisition and use for self-development of subject matter not easily susceptible to the marketplace rationalizations of the larger society; and an unwillingness of that larger society to encourage schools in the process of environmental democratization by allowing them to educate for self-development *and* social efficiency, rather than for the latter alone. These conditions cannot fail to work against the necessary and well-recognized need for individualization of learning on a scale matching the scale of environmental social needs themselves.

Truly, as a segment of the managerial class in formal education has already realized, individualizing learning within the confines of a system largely rationalized from outside, and doing so in ways that improve both the functioning of the system and the total life-format of the individual learner means defining and operating within a whole new set of parameters in management. Balancing a school budget or maneuvering successive classes into higher group test scores cannot any longer constitute goals in themselves; they will be relegated to a more appropriate place lower in the list of priorities. The human and social costs of formal schooling, like those of any other group undertaking in an interdependent society, must now be much more carefully studied and given fuller advance consideration.

Democratization in education complements the environmental democratization slowly overtaking society as a whole. It is not at all a matter of accident that the more advanced minds in education are most concerned with defining and making operational the concept of equality in learning. The essence of social responsibility for education in an environmental era will consist in providing for individual needs on a mass basis, rather than merely in maintaining a minimum opportunity structure in which an elite can be siphoned off from a baser by-product, which is left a kind of human dross condemned to compete and suffer inevitable defeat both in the brief period of formal schooling and in the real-life struggle that follows.

In previous chapters, for this reason, the stress has been on what better kinds of education could be provided for the *average* child, adolescent, youth, and adult. This was not a matter of focusing on special programs for the potentially upward mobile (e.g., gifted children in elementary schools, intellectually early achievers funneled into high school and college honors courses, bright young workers recruited into career training programs of such corporations with advanced educational interests as RCA or IBM). Rather, the intended focus has been upon the common citizen of whatever age, in his educational pursuits. Interlocking or successive elites may govern a modern society; they do not constitute it, and what happens to mass humanity will determine how well or how inadequately social-environmental goals are reached, not what becomes of this or that temporary elite. It is the elites that are school-oriented; common humanity sees and will in future see formal education only as a means to bettering its grasp on the shifting, stressful business of daily life.

Thus the core problems of a phase-in to environmental social living, in an intermediate period of decades just ahead when men must adjust individually and socially to changing patterns of existence, center on the mass psyche and its potential for adaptation. For the present and near-future, one key indicator of success or failure in their adaptation to change must be the mass reaction to our swiftly emerging energy-resources crisis. The social rifts and problems already created by this crisis are worth a brief examination here.

As early-day observers of the industrial scene (e.g., Henry Adams) noted as long ago as the beginning of this century, Western cultures have been evolving toward contemporary stages of development through a centuries-long social process in which ever greater efficiency in the exploitation of energy resources has been matched only too fortuitously by an increasing level of demand. Energy as the prime mover of any society can be drawn from two sources: the physical environment or from man himself. Those societies which still depend to a large extent on brute manpower to get the major share of necessary work accomplished are by definition less developed than those which harness nature for these tasks. Every society, developed or underdeveloped, aims to maximize its natural energy resources and diminish the need for unrewarding and physically destructive hard labor by humans in the necessary business of social life. This trend has been in existence long enough so that now its drawbacks on a world scale are becoming apparent.

So long as more natural energy could be produced than was needed or used by the population of a society proceeding with the mission of its own development, the mark of its culture was its moral confidence in a social philosophy of material growth. Western cultures provide the clearest examples. They granted to the individual a right, perhaps even a duty, steadily to expand his autonomy over both physical and social environments and, in doing so, to make use of energy from any available source at a constantly increasing rate. In a world now populated by some 3.8 billion humans, and with population expanding at rates unfortunately high, man as primarily an energy consumer can only come more and more to interfere with all rational planning for future social welfare.

The skill and adaptability that the race can show in dealing with this problem will reveal its potential for handling the many lesser problems of a socioeconomic-learning nature that entry into an environmental age will pose. To date, people are tending to see the energy-resources issue, nevertheless, as a primarily partisan matter, a political and economic argument, in which the only possible reaction is to take sides and join in a knock-down contest for individual and small-group advantage. Its significance as a world problem divorced from "adversary context" and as a learning experience for a people nearly at the point of entry to an environmental social status is largely lost.

Thus ecologists are pitted against big business interests in what has all the appearance of a battle to the death, with government serving as a presumably impartial referee. One hears those points of view which describe nothing more than the particular special interests of the two sides *as adversaries*. In point of fact, these exchanges are essentially old-style legal arguments that tend in the unhappier cases to elicit a self-serving extremism from both sides, a situation only too reminiscent of the continuing and intractable opposition between extreme Left and extreme Right in modern national and international politics.

What is lost in all such verbal fireworks is the real interest of mass humanity. This interest can no longer be served by laissez-faire policies toward so vital a resource as energy. Government management of energy production and use becomes daily more imperative.[4] The Western cultural ideal of endless economic growth and its counterpart of a society given over to endless sybaritic high-consumption behavior are playing out. Man's energy supply is seriously faltering and he has not yet found a new system of belief to replace the one built on the principle of energy from nature as an unfailing resource. Man cannot now turn back; he can but move on through time into an uncertain future, knowing that "faiths built only on Western foundations are, by definition, inadequate for the challenge posed by the energy dilemma."[5] So then, there will be stress, turmoil, shortages, insecurity, and uncertain management from above, all in the course of adjustment by humankind to a drastic turnaround in the culture of energy consumption. This crisis is the prototype for all future social-environmental learning. How can mass humanity be taught why change is necessary and how can man, the individual, be taught to accept change of such proportions.

Social Learning: The Social Basis

Assume that by a fortuitous chain of events it became possible for "people" living on Planet X to communicate with us on earth. This might take place in the last years of the present century or the early years of the next century. Planet X is many light years distant from earth, located in a far galaxy, but the state of radio communications technology by the late 1990s permits fairly continuous interchange of conversation between X and ourselves. After the discovery of one another and following a period of adjustment to the languages and thought forms of earth people, the more advanced inhabitants of X, beings more similar to men on earth than science fiction might have led us to believe, display a certain interest in studying the problems of their cosmic "neighbors." One of earth's leading philosophers of education has the following Platonic exchange with a savant from X:

X-man: As you describe your system and as our machines monitor the data your machines have provided, it seems the case that in your earthly societies nearly every behavior of your people involves some kind of calculation of results that meet a precondition. That is, you earthmen spend all your waking moments, by and large, in efforts to control future events, especially physical ones. Your every action is directed to this attempt to manage the future. Particularly your institutions are more and more geared to exert forms of management over your people. But management of future behavior does not seem to work out very well for you at all. To us this whole way of proceeding seems puzzling, indeed. You do not learn from experience. You impose constraints in ever increasing number, but your social conditions do not by your own admission really improve. Your people behave as if the theory of behavior management were one with its practice, and clearly it is not . . . .

Earthman: You are embarrassingly correct in your judgment. But consider the scope of our problems. We are a fast-increasing species, unable to control very well our own growth rates. And great masses of earth dwellers live in ignorance of the effects of their behavior, either upon themselves or upon our planet. Yet as our social life becomes more complex and as earthly society becomes more diverse or pluralistic — some would say more fragmented — we appear to have no choice other than to exert those controls which would seem to maintain minimum conditions of social stability.

X-man: What you are saying is that your people are essentially unable at this stage to govern themselves.

Earthman: That would be a fairly accurate appraisal of our present situation. But we do recognize the problem. What we lack is a broad enough view of future possibilities. It is with this in mind that I have been put in contact with you. We hope that from your experience we might gain some better ideas of alternative policies or directions.

X-man: Yes. I understand. Of course, we here on X have a quite different biological and a very different social history. It is hard to draw parallels. We worry little over controlling future events because, I suppose, our race is so constituted physically and socially that only a narrow range of future behaviors is possible. Frankly, we have come to prefer it that way, although it was not always so.

Earthman: But this is just what matters to us on earth. A race of highly intelligent beings such as yours to have arrived at your present state of social development must earlier have undergone certain critical experiences. Couldn't we profit from knowing more about those events?

X-man: Yes, perhaps . . . . (There is a long pause here, and then the voice from outer space goes on.) It is true that we were at something like your present social level a dozen-odd generations ago, give or take some few differences in customs. But even for us at that time general conditions were hardly the same as yours now. X has a floral and mineral status far different from earth's. From the very first, food and energy needs of our society have been very difficult to meet. This has meant a dissimilar social development, both in its pace and from a qualitative point of view. Our history reveals none of your continuous development of technology primarily to serve a small upper class holding total ownership of the means of production. We passed through the slave-holding

stage quickly and without lasting ill effects. Our physical
evolution also has made us rather more placid as animals
than you earth dwellers, with your warmer blood. We have
never in our history possessed the physical means of maintaining a large population. Too, we are of one race only. All
in all, we are in balance — now.

Earthman: Still, in spite of all these differences you mention, there are similarities. Your people experienced certain
times of great difficulty. Can you explain what happened in
your society those dozen generations ago?

X-man: I hesitate to discuss this, because for all your need
you may draw unreasonably fixed conclusions . . . (A long
pause occurs. Then the X-man continues.) You see, our
problem was faced at a time when conditions for solution
were propitious. You on earth have not yet attained those
conditions, and that may make for different outcomes. There
is this gap between theory and practice, as witness developments in your earthly communist societies since the revolution in Russia. Still . . . . (Once more the voice from outer
space trails off, then after a cosmic pause begins again.) Well,
if I can sum up, our situation was this: we had been living
with a system of private rights guaranteed more by custom
than by any legal code — rights to property, privacy, and
association. We were a society small in numbers, a phlegmatic,
unassuming people, not too curious about new pleasures and
little given to a range of passions such as those you earthmen
suffer. We had by a series of happy discoveries been able to
mechanize most of the basic production techniques needed
to sustain life at a suitable level of comfort. We have had no
need then or since for the elaborate division of labor you
require on earth. Those who cared to spent more time in
technological pursuits, but they did so not with the desire
to achieve personal gain. They were content to use their
talents for the improvement of public welfare — all, that is,
save for a few. And these few did pose a recognizable
problem, which had to be dealt with. We were at that time
developing an advanced computer capability, something

you are just now approaching on earth. This was perhaps a fortunate coincidence. Our population, always relatively small, was well educated, at least for those times. It was a society capable of exercising group judgment. With the aid of our high-speed computers, we could act to regulate all external social life and do so in the final best interests of everyone, based on what to you even with your presently emerging computer science would seem an infinity and a perhaps pointless melange of quantifiable factors. The question, which every member of society recognized as basic, had to do with the effects on our entire body social of certain activities carried on by individuals, a question of how and at whose expense the individual could rightly grow and express himself. Unlike the members of your earthly societies, our people did not shrink from accepting the necessity for deciding how this question should be answered.

Earthman: You created a wholly regulated society? (He gives a whistle of mild astonishment.) But then you also took away from people the challenge of the unknown. You reduced everything in life to a certainty. Where this has been attempted on earth it has only increased the suicide rate and made human beings more sullen and contemptuous of organized society. (He realizes he has jumped ahead of his interlocuter.) But excuse me, I am breaking in upon your story. Will you go on? What happened on X? How did *you* work out the problem?

X-man: I have perhaps overemphasized the differences between our society then and yours now. (He chuckles with something akin to human good nature.) But there were some similarities, too. We had citizens who in their mild way sought to manipulate other people to secure their private ends. In an environment with very limited resources such activities become dangerous, as you know. There was a need to bring about changes.

Earthman (prodding gently, as the X-man again hesitates): So you underwent something like one of our earthly revolutions . . . .

X-man: In a manner of speaking, yes. A revolution, but a rather quiet one by your standards. Our leaders, if you could call them that, recognized this need to act. They canvassed the people. Widespread agreement on a certain essential point was obtained: that our judgments as animal beings, taken singly or collectively, were less dependable than those of our computers in the matter of regulation of group life. It was agreed that the system of representative political parties, a system which perpetuated rather than diminished clevages in our society, was too expensive to maintain side by side with an advanced computer capacity. We turned our problem of governance and regulation of private external activity, by common consent, over to our machines.

Earthman (disguising his mixed horror and fascination by holding his voice firm): And how did this work itself out?

X-man: Again, I sense your haste to draw from our experiences certain conclusions with regard to your own society. I hesitate to go on. But then, the story is simply enough told. Our machines laid out a plan by which to eradicate all unnecessary remaining division of labor, differences in ownership of wealth, and social-class distinctions such as they were over a four-generation span. Accept what I say in this regard carefully, of course, because the process of which I am speaking was very dissimilar from what has happened on earth when, say, Marxist revolutionaries have taken over a capitalist society. With our then high level of computer technology and our small, homogeneous population, you see, a plan could be laid out which solved our major problems really well in advance. To be sure, we had to give up any expectation that everything could be accomplished in one generation. If we had been unwilling to accept this, our computers would have reminded us of it in the strongest terms. They told us, in fact, that we must begin with our children. And we must work with those children not so much methodically as provocatively. Do you follow me?

Earthman: I am not sure I do . . . .

X-man: Well, in essence we transformed everything that

had a bearing on how our children might come to view life. Being a people small in number, we could take steps to provide resources for special pre-school experiences. Then we completely reorganized our schools to make them serve the purpose that had been agreed on: to build citizens able to accommodate both as young people and as adults to a way of life in which externals *must* be subordinated to internals. This was of course not such a difficult task for us as it might be for you earth people. At least, we seem to have succeeded fairly well. Our whole society now operates on the principle of individual self-development in the pursuit of social goals. We no longer strive wastefully to regulate the individual's future activities because we have achieved a successful regulation of *society's* future activities. Our people, in short, are all too dependable and properly conditioned in self-discipline for us to have to worry about the shape of the future. In any event, our latest generation of computers has elaborated, within extremely broad limits, all possible future events and combinations of events, even including the destruction of our solar system, and we are, I can say without boasting, in a position to control our social destiny more or less totally.

Earthman: You make it sound so easy. Here on earth, I fear, we have not had your luck in the pattern of our development. And we lack some quality you people seem to possess in plenty — what might be called social fortitude, the ability to take race survival more or less for granted. But be that as it may. What I am wondering about now is how you managed your schools to achieve this goal of making your children accept the priority of internal life.

X-man: Yes, I can understand your curiosity on that point. The best way I can describe what happened, it seems to me, would be to say that those schools ceased to be what you earth people now and we then traditionally might consider schools. They became instead what you today would call the leading edge in social and intellectual life. Schools were permitted to develop freely, not maintained as institutions controlled from without. Without going into all the detail of our history during that time, I can simply state that our children and youth were raised in three or four generations from a status of neophyte-dependents to one of neophyte-equals in the social process. Do you follow me?

Earthman: But what of the adults? Didn't they have problems?

X-man: Yes. However, these were not so serious as you might imagine, from your earth person's point of view. Our atmosphere, you will recall, is thinner here. We live on a lesser amount of oxygen, and over the millennia this has affected our bodily adaptations. Our bodily structures, as you know, differ somewhat from yours. We lack a number of elements that seem to make you earth people more volatile in behavior — adrenal glands, a high metabolism rate, energy surplus. We are not able to hurry or get along with little sleep or become so vastly preoccupied over sex. We do not tend toward strong reactions over anything. Nor is this all a matter of differences in physical environment and consequent differential adaptations. We have a much longer history: sixteen thousand years as a highly socialized, yet aculturally reasoning species on this planet, as compared to your four or five thousand on earth. Simply by virtue of this greater passage of time we can expect to have better succeeded in controlling what can be controlled and in living with what cannot be so controlled. You earth people have accumulated many problems that we luckily have never had to face. Yours is a situation we do not envy, being complicated by variables which we have never encountered. I wish it were possible for me to advise you with some degree of confidence, but under the circumstances it would be unjustifiably presumptuous.

Earthman: But you would be willing to pass on to us further data and details of this phase of your social development — so we can at least draw our own conclusions?

X-man: Certainly. And if there is any piece of advice I might give, it would be that you earth people not underestimate the learning capabilities of your species. Your society cannot refine itself, any more than ours did, without massive learning to support new modes of behavior — behavior that is socially understood and approved.

Earthman: We thank you for your help. It may not make our task easier, but it allows us the better to keep to a sensible course as we negotiate our myriad difficulties.

X-man: Peace, and fellowship. We here on X wish you well.

A Final Word: Toward A Morality of Environmental Education

An education for life in the coming environmental age must be an education for adaptation. But until our goal of learning, the specification of what is meant by "adaptation," is made clear, we have no basis for any educational prescriptions. The adaptation often spoken of above is not to be thought of as merely *adjustment*, the sum of simple, primarily physical reactions of an animal to a milieu perceived in animal terms of reference. This would not, at our late stage of intellectual and social development as a species, constitute significant adaptation, at least in a basically human context.

Nevertheless, adaptation, in the environmental sense, does begin from the assumption of a successful adjustment to essential creature needs. The environmentally adapted human being is already in control of hunger, thirst, sex, and socialization drives, in control, that is, to the extent that he can accept considerable deflection of these drives from time to time, can sublimate them where necessary in the interest of longer-term, more significant priorities. The converse of this dictum is that the environmentally adapted human has a firm set, regardless of whether or not he qualifies as a bona fide "intellectual," toward the use of inner resources to promote personal growth, (This is not, however, an exact restatement of the Jungian dichotomy between introvert and extrovert, with a superior value placed upon the former. In the environmental point of view, the developmental and evolutionary needs of the individual are stressed in relation to emerging patterns of socioenvironmental constraint. Thus adaptation, to be successful, presupposes a *balance*, unique to the individual, between the ability to develop inner resources and an ability to develop coping mechanisms to deal with the problems of external, daily living.)

Further, the adapted person has a tolerant attitude toward the social behavior he regards as dubious in value and a hopeful, cooperative attitude toward the social behavior he feels is aiding mankind in moving the race in the direction of essential change. He must have a sensitivity to his own place in a complex•social order. Above all, he holds his own person of value irrespective of social conditions about him, yet he quite willingly works to achieve not only his own optimum adaptation within his environment but also that of those other persons in his orbit of social functioning.

In specifying this groundwork for a theory of successful adaptation in the coming environmental age, one of course assumes the risks that accompany any attempt to state philosophical generalizations that would encompass all manifestations of behavior in a complex setting (becoming, incidentally, more complex daily and even hourly). This attempt is made much more necessary, however, by the knowledge that in an already over-populated world, restriction and necessity constantly act to limit human behavior in its more destructive expression. In this sense of behavioral limits, any environmental philosophy for the late-twentieth-century world is a genuine extension of Herbert Spencer's philosophy of behavior based on social Darwinism: there are mathematically determined courses of behavior and adaptation that, *sui generis,* provide any given individual the best modes of life maintenance, and logic dictates that no effort be spared to ascertain these courses and follow them.

One pertinent criticism that will be advanced is that the above view of man's relation to the sociophysical universe is no more than a modernized version of the Greek Stoic philosophy and is placed in opposition to a contemporary and ubiquitous Epicureanism, which is the sybaritic expression of today's colossal distrust by the individual of any society that seeks actively to control or direct his overt animal behavior. Seen from this standpoint, the environmental ethic is no more than another philosophy of anchoritism of fatalism that leaves the individual no further advanced today in ordering his *own* fate than was the Greek of 450 B.C., except that he is living in an era of more sophisticated technology. But this view overlooks the factor of historical necessity, the gradually emerging need for integration implicit in the concept of applied environmentalism or in the construct of environmentalism as a governing mode of universal behavior.

In an era of environmental crisis, when the power of technology has finally forced man to concede the permanent and anterior significance of his own actions in the maintenance of a balance of life forces within the global milieu, the individual is faced with a challenge more direct and more psychologically demanding than any presented in the past. To survive with meaning, he must now integrate not only socially but also individually — with his fellows and within himself. He must strike a point of positive psychic balance, one that allows him to serve *himself* optimally at the same time that he serves in the broadest sense both his society and his physical environment. This goal goes beyond the popularized extremes of modern Stoicism and Epicureanism. It renews in a wholly contemporary sense the classic Socratic search for significant living. Yet this occurs in a social and intellectual atmosphere quite unlike that of Greece of the Golden Age, when despite a unique standard of artistic excellence technology had not escaped the bonds of an essentially benighted and ultra-religious ethos, when inequality of opportunity was naturally assumed in all human undertakings, when the heroic *individual* outwardly struggling against a remorseless destiny symbolized the ultimate social crucible of behavior, and when the problems of a *mass* democratic society were as yet undreamed of.

Modern society faces many problems at the operational

level, problems that have their base in social lag on the educational and communications fronts, but, in the broadest theoretical sense, the one overriding problem is that of participation. The relatively small socioeconomic elites of advanced society have yet to join with the striving under-privileged or disadvantaged masses to participate in the work that social evolution entails. This work is necessarily more than a matter of funding various give-away projects to distribute excess wealth to ghetto dwellers and more than acceptance by the power structure and general public of even a well-conceived scheme to break the poverty-ignorance cycle at its source (e.g., the "Freedom Budget for All Americans" put forth by A. Philip Randolph, a radical plan to reshape the federal budget so as to funnel billions of dollars out of the "continuously expanding" U.S. economy into urban human rehabilitation programs[6]).

Participation, rather, must take form primarily as a self-less, nonmaterialistic, and morally needful sharing, a sharing among those whose treasure consists not of political power and external control of wealth but in a mentality steeped in the spirit of positive social and interpersonal criticism. Too, such a spirit cannot exist in a vacuum of individualism, apart from the general flow of social inter-course. It may even have to depend on beginnings in simple models and prototypes on which person-to-person behavior could be based. The formal educator could provide one important personal behavioral model and the school an im-portant institutional model. But the spirit of sharing that any true environmental philosophy presupposes must primarily evolve, as a culture itself evolves, with the implicit consent of the people whose lives it will affect.

The first generations of our post-industrial society have been obsessed with efficiency, specialization, expansion, quantification of results, individual aggrandizement, competi-tion without regard to consequences when this principle is pursued to its theoretical limits, and the continuous ration-alization of social and economic processess for too narrowly prescribed purposes. Even the Christian ethic has had to be commercialized to a degree by churches hard pressed to survive in a milieu of conflicting interests. But there indisputably remain the urge to charity toward others and control over oneself as the residual virtues of all ethical systems and of the historically established religions themselves, and it is no accident that these directions in which the mature human will inclines are also the bases of any environmentally appropriate behavior for the indefinite future. The core of the historical religions provides in its substance, if not in its ritualistic forms, nearly all needed moral content suitable to the learner's use. The problem consists in transforming this content into experiences promoting the desired learning in a totally contemporary society.

An environmentally behaving adult is the product, in large part, of an education that prepares him to adapt in the present and at the same time sets him further along the path of positive future adaptation. Present conditions in both the formal school and in the outer society seem less than wholly advantageous to optimum adaptive learning. Both society and the individual bear a degree of responsibility for this situation. Competitive (socioeconomically but not humanistically rationalized) modern societies have worked to distort the natural balance of forces that make up the human psyche in the interest of attaining oversimplified goals prescribed by inadequately informed policy-setting elites. The individual, having allowed himself to develop too negative an image of his relationship to society, lacks the restraints needed to maintain adequate internal controls over behavior stimulated by events in the external environment. Again, the problem is one of social lag and nonintegration. The old society cannot move out of its historical shell of evolution-defying conservatism so long as a majority of those with an influence over the course of events maintain their existing social attitude, i.e., that *ipso facto* the common citizen cannot be trusted to participate without positive *external* pressures in an ordered social process. Yet even the present situation offers possibilities for future development, although clearly — with the industrialized society's negation of the individual and his forced compliance in a system of largely unreflected behaviors — it also marks no more than a fairly well defined halfway station in the evolution of human group-living processes toward a condition of far more environmental constancy and balance.

This present-day situation in no way serves to contradict once and for all the long-term participatory ideal of an environmental society. It merely constitutes a barrier, and a real one, to quick passage into that stage of social living when balance between the human and his environment at last becomes supremely possible. Adaptive education is the tool by which best to bridge this barrier. Then the learning process, too, in a futurist society, must become more complex than in earlier days: one in which intellection, the straining of every cognitive resource to ascertain the limits of reality and determine optimum reactions to that reality, *must* be supplemented by usable affective resources. Through his control over affective states, the full emotional powers of the individual will be marshaled to balance his behavior in society's interest while bolstering him in his own self-esteem.

For this reason, and again the point must be well stressed, the individual's education cannot be considered apart from its affective component. In the environmental view affective development is more than the maintenance of that drug-induced state of semi-somnolence which so appeals to today's immature mind because it shuts off the more troublesome aspects of daily life. It is a development that constantly confirms and renews, by a kind of perpetual exchange of interpersonal understanding about the moral obligations of man, those values which make effective individual adaptation possible: social conscience; self-reliance; the will to persevere; self-respect; and the genuine desire to make one's own way without compromising oneself or others. In specifying the contemporary primacy of these ancient values, however, one cannot also hold to any by-now-inap-

propriate simplicity of mind such as that of certain of the
early Christian saints, especially those who disdained study
and the application of logical thought to sociomoral problems and sought refuge in prayer and contemplation solely.
This ineffectual blankness of mind of the *coeur simple* is
an inversion of that receptive affective state which in contemporary and future society is needed for maximum individual
self-development in an environmental·social context.

I am not necessarily speaking of these values as being part
and parcel of the state of awareness of the individual. Such
values may exist only as a set of desiderata in the minds of
a small minority of people in any society, even a relatively
advanced one. As has previously been pointed out, the
ability to bring to functional awareness essential environmental values does not come automatically. Most humans,
given the directed character of their existence or their backward conditions of life, proceed from birth to death without
attaining significant awareness of the *value* component of
their situations. Any program of education for an advanced
human society must encompass the task of developing and
magnifying the sum total of such awareness. But the assumption that mankind can wait for a majority of individuals to
reach this desired state of mental openness stands in open
contradiction to what is universally foreseen as a hard struggle
for social development over the intervening decades until a
distinctly environmental human order can become operative.

Modern education, therefore, has the further task of
structuring, through its total effect on a population, the conditions of life — for those who attain or will attain awareness
as well as those who do not or will not — so as to permit
society to continue evolving as directly as possible toward its
point of optimum environmental balance. This will mean, as
has already been stated in various contexts, that in some
degree any valid education must lead the person in the direction of full control over the self, over both the conscious and
the unconscious mind. Thus, when one considers the goal of
an adaptive education, he must accord prior place to those

experiences which help the individual optimize in an environmental (not a purely personal) sense some chosen combination of future growth possibilities and aid him in deflecting or psychologically neutralizing potentially destructive experiential possibilities.

In a civilization advanced in technology, where everyone both teaches and learns, where a whole environment in all its diversity educates, yet where the individual on the receiving end of this vast con.ɔlex of stimuli has only limited powers of discernment and judgment, he learns cognitively as well as affectively, through subliminal means as well as via ratiocinative processes. Even those who teach consciously are bound by the limits that the complications of life in an advanced society impose. Fortunately, the teacher can hew to his one overriding goal, the shaping of men for adaptive fulfillment in a future society based on environmental truths. Such a teacher is therefore shaping not only a reasoning power but, even more, a set of attitudes: toward self, toward others, toward the physical surroundings one has lifelong contact with, and toward life itself. With a goal of such importance, a very great range of means to goal attainment can be brought under consideration. Indeed, it may be that many of the vexing moral problems that accompany the use of certain means for attaining educational goals today will fairly soon, given recognition of the significance of the greater goal that will by then have been universally set, cease to burden the minds of men.

Equally, it seems not impossible that, even in our much-derided contemporary school curriculum, the problem of subject matter will not pose such insuperable difficulties as has been thought. In the specialized society no one can avoid the onus of at least external conformity to specialized pursuits. This has suggested to innumerable people caught up in the demands of a technological society that "historically irrelevant" studies must ultimately disappear from the program of any formal school. But the mere continued presence in the contemporary curriculum of such subjects as art or music, however mechanically these may be taught, serves to remind us that no matter what the degree of dominance of technology throughout a society, men do continue to need the freedom provided by experiences of less rational or less channeled creative pursuits. While the question of balance within an environmentally grounded curriculum constitutes a separate subject of discussion, it may be said (with fear of contradiction only from those who have swallowed whole the fiction of man's need to follow blindly wherever technology leads) that the balanced human being who has *adapted* to environmental imperatives is not lacking in those graces and attainments which have traditionally set apart cultivated from uncultivated men and that an environmental education must provide appropriate experiences of a cultural (as opposed to an exclusively technical) nature.

Beyond this, and implied in it, remains the issue of the ideal of humanity that this newly emerging world of environmental checks and balances suggests. This ideal cannot be based on futurism alone, ignoring millennia of past traditions and values so laboriously attained. Future man will be different in many ways from the man of today, for to adapt means to accept change and adjust successfully to that change. But future man will also find it necessary in a historical sense to remain what he has already become. This supreme balancing act requires the maintenance and refinement of the higher human capacities, requires selecting those cultural traits which are of superior importance in environmental social evolution. In the maintaining, refinement, and selection, leadership and example are just as likely as in past joint human enterprises to remain the elements of success *sine qua non*.

This is a point against which, in the maelstrom of contemporary life, with its radical social and intellectual divisions within any advanced society, much unnecessary and destructive effort is expended. The sense of change can become so strong as to blind one to the importance of maintaining a still-valid heritage. The traditions of leadership and example, both Western and non-Western, continue to be useful; they are in fact essential components of any successful, future, mass social adaptation. Men look forward and backward at the same time, assessing a heritage even as they transmute it in immediate forms of action in the light of emerging new necessities of behavior. In particular, the moral tradition will constitute an *a priori* major social need in the environmentalized society. The moral force or power of each manifestation of higher humanistic leadership or example will indeed form the key affective impulse behind vital environmental learning.

The ideal of humanity for this coming age, too, blends imperceptibly with the major goal of an environmental education: the fulfillment of a human being in light of his own and his milieu's requirements, an evolved human being in an evolved society, one who has the capacity to blend the best of past and present in his behavior and who carries the behavior of the future "in his bones." This is as yet a dream, but a dream that would break down (in a realistic as well as a theoretical sense) the Rousseauian dichotomy between man and society. This dream expresses a hope that men have a right to maintain: that the society of tomorrow can achieve a balance between internal and external forces, between its legal or cultural mandates and the actual will of the masses to fulfill them. If the previous discussions in this book augur anything for man's future on this planet, there is only one direction the race can take in making this hope a reality: toward third-stage individual-social evolution, toward race-wide accommodation, however gradually achieved, to environmental imperatives — within the self, within society, and between society and the planetary support system.

It may reasonably be argued that the moral force of such an integrated society would overwhelm today's self-conscious, effect-seeking, as yet psychically underdeveloped average man. This interpretation is no doubt not far from accurate. But regardless of the debility of today's social enterprise, the evolutionary direction of human group living must be acknowledged. In tomorrow's world nothing will seem more natural than to accept an integrated society as the essential base from which more important business — the individual's self-development — can better be carried forward.

Today's man, an intermediate type, seeks tentatively for a foothold on the path leading to that future state of positive adaptation. He does so as any learner would, with an inadequate but growing knowledge: of himself, of his society, of the universe as it spreads out toward infinity from its point of beginning in his own body and brain. He inhabits an uncomfortable present, looking back with some rue at a past that he has shaped rather incongruously and in many ways to such seemingly destructive ends. He vacillates nervously between inordinate pessimism and perhaps unreasonable hope as he views a future sure to involve constant, unavoidable, and often tumultuous change. Is it any wonder that a poet of today should have titled his major work *The Age of Anxiety?*

Given this situation, how can the average adult of today work out for himself some fairly satisfying path of behavior, much less the average child? The question is a hard one. In fact, the average child may be, from the standpoint of his opportunities for learning through the institutional framework of education over the next several decades, in a better way than the average adult. Educational theorists have already laid out in conceptual form curricular structures that, given suitable implementation, could maximize learning opportunities within the existing system of bureaucratized schooling.[7] In saying this, I am not writing off the importance of adult education in the critical final decades of the twentieth century. But there must be acknowledged the tremendous and in great part unformulatable difficulties that face, as the existential philosophers have made so abundantly evident, contemporary adults in their efforts to adapt to the environmentally dictated conditions of future life.

Perhaps it is both natural and inevitable that the child will always have a place of prior importance in the educational scheme of things. It must then be equally natural and inevitable that people look to the school as a viable tool in the shaping of those who will inhabit and adapt to the future society of an environmental era. Earlier some suggestions were given for moving the school into a position of greater autonomy as a social institution. This was a radical step, one proposed seriously as a hopefully valid alternative to a system of education seemingly less and less suited, as time passes, to the swiftly building new needs of environmental society. The question is not so much one of what schools have failed to accomplish in their long historical development to the present. Instead, it is one of how quickly they are falling behind with their inflexibility and inability to alter traditional practices, in the struggle to equip new generations for future group life. The problem is not localized or limited to specific cultures. There has been a relative uniformity in recent generations in the development of formal schooling practices across the international spectrum. In light of the restricted nature of their social mission, schools in the developed countries are probably already at a state of near-maximum efficiency in performance. The recognition is growing increasingly that schools cannot singlehandedly remake or integrate fragmented, still only partly evolved societies. But they are part of a universal process and, as their function is integrated ever more closely with the conscious social direction of that process, they can better contribute to a continuing evolution that society as a whole can in no event choose to avoid.

An education of the total society to new values and more integrative behaviors remains the primary, all-inclusive, and indeed absolute prior goal of any realistic program of learning arising out of the environmental point of view. In our strenuous attempts to cope and cope again, we are in effect shaping a future society on the basis of accumulated interpretations of every shred of past experience. This experience, even in its variety, points to certain particular avenues of future development and suggests certain imperatives of behavior for the coming environmental age - and to these imperatives the individual must be made more adaptable, more sensitive, more dedicated. To secure this end the individual will be given a wider range of learning opportunities than men have had or have needed before.

Many elements of the new education will develop naturally, in the inevitably *ad hoc* recognition of needs or concerns not seen in advance. But planning for this education and for the behavior it is expected to produce cannot be skimped in any wise, especially at the level of highest human achievement. There must therefore be a stress on the teaching and learning of values. It is appropriate that my final comment should concern the dual nature of value transmission. One learns values directly, at the conscious intellectual level. One also learns them subliminally through the mesh of interpersonal experiences, in the process of social exchange, by psychic osmosis, so to say.

Even in the radically changed society of tomorrow, it should not be forgotten, the young will meet and absorb the influence of the old, the neophyte will learn from the person of experience. A continuing, even growing, significance will attach for this reason to the exemplary behavior of those who, by chance or by design, are cast in the roles of guides to learning. To the tyro a respected guide will reflect, then as now, consciously or unconsciously, the best of which an imperfect race is capable. For this phenomenon to have the kind of effect suggested, a movement to "environmentalize" the species through learning model behavior must take place. The process is of the same degree of complexity as the learning process itself, but it requires the additional complication of seeking new ways of opening minds and psyches, worldwide, to the breadth and depth of human potential.

> If we, as ordinary educators, whose task . . . is to transmit from [the] enrichers of life [the geniuses of human creativity] their wisdom to the unformed turbulent future, to transform reflection into action consonant with their thought, then some of their luminosity must encompass our minds; their passion must, in degree, break through our opaque thoughts and descend to us.[8]

This is the educator's task. It is a challenge to man's spirit and staying power. It is a challenge that can, like all the great challenges to man down through history, be met and surmounted.

References

Chapter 1

1. Pierre Lecomte du Noüy, *Human Destiny,* (New York: Longmans, Green, 1947).

2. Friedrich Nietzsche, *The Use and Abuse of History,* trans. Adrian Collins. (New York and Indianapolis: Bobbs-Merrill, 1957).

3. Christopher Jencks, *Inequality: A Reassessment of the Effect of Family and Schooling in America.* (New York: Basic Books, 1972).

4. Calvin W. Stillman, "Reflections on Environmental Education," *Teachers College Record* 74, no. 2 (Dec. 1972): 196.

5. This issue of the link-up between the student's "world out there" and what is "learned" in the school setting is a developing concern of the community of educators and is leading to consideration of alternatives (sometimes radical) to the traditional modes of formal instruction. In this connection it is germane to quote the answers that children have given one investigator when he posed the question, "What could schools do to educate you in ways that no other agencies could or should?" The major answers were as follows:

1) Provide a framework or system around what is learned in school to insure understanding. Nothing is more useless than a lot of disconnected content items that can't be fitted together.
2) Teach "fundamentals." The tools needed for thinking and serving can be gained only in school.
3) Give opportunities and materials for inquiry, discovery, and the probing of meaning. Nothing is more important in the school years than getting at the meaning of things.
4) "Stop attempting to compete with and to destroy what we learn elsewhere. Instead, seek to coordinate what we are taught in school with what we learn outside school."

Based on Ronald C. Doll, "Alternative Forms of Schooling," *Educational Leadership* 29, no. 5 (Feb. 1972): 392.

Chapter 2

1. *Time Magazine,* "Fighting to Save the Earth from Man," February 2, 1970, p. 4.

2. R. W. Comstock, "Man and his Environment: One Industrial Point of View," *The Science Teacher* 37, no. 6 (Sept. 1970): 24.

3. See especially René Dubos, *Science Looks at Itself,* Introduction (New York: Scribner, 1970). Of pertinence in the same volume may be found Roy A. Rappaport, "Purpose, Property, and Environmental Disaster," pp. 5-9.

4. Garrett Hardin, "The Tragedy of the Commons," *Science,* December 13, 1968. Reprinted in Mary E. Hawkins, ed., *Vital Views of the Environment.* Washington, D.C.: National Science Teachers Association (1970), p. 5.

5. Comstock, p. 25.

Chapter 3

1. Reference is made to the situation well-known to operations analysts and researchers, that of the "statistical decision error of the third kind," i.e., an error that consists of solving a problem that is the wrong one on which to be working. See I. I. Mitroff and Frederick Betz, "Dialectical Decision Theory: A Meta-Theory of Decision-Making," *Management Science* 19, no. 1 (Sept. 1972): 11-24.

2. See A. H. Maslow, *Motivation and Personality* (New York: Harper, 1954). See also Frank G. Goble, *The Third Force — The Psychology of Abraham Maslow* (New York: Grossman/Viking, 1970).

3. Charles Darwin, *Origin of Species.* Harvard Classics Ed. vol. 11 (New York: Collier. 1937).

4. See Vance Packard, *Nation of Strangers* (New York: McKay, 1972).

5. Van Cleve Morris, *Philosophy and the American School* (Boston: Houghton Mifflin, 1961), p. 90.

6. Some apropos and interesting comments regarding the problems of motivation and social cohesion within differing sociopolitical contexts (e.g., U.S.A., Nazi Germany, Soviet Russia, etc.) are offered in J. K. Galbraith, *The New Industrial State* (New York: New American Library, 1967), pp. 109-19, 150-56.

7. See Galbraith, chap. 1, "Change and the Industrial System" and his earlier work, *The Affluent Society* (Boston: Houghton Mifflin, 1958).

8. Alexander Solzhenitsyn, *Nobel Lecture,* trans. F. D. Reeve (New York: Farrar, Straus & Giroux, 1972).

9. See Colin Greer, *The Great School Legend: a Revisionist Interpretation of American Public Education* (New York: Basic Books, 1972). See also Christopher Jencks, *Inequality: A Reassessment of the Effect of Family and Schooling in America* (New York: Basic Books, 1972).

10. Kenneth Eells *et al., Intelligence and Cultural Differences: A Study of Cultural Learning and Problem Solving* (Chicago: University of Chicago Press, 1951), pp. 154-58. See also Allison Davis, "The Educability of the Children of the Poor," in United States Office of Education, *The Unfinished Journey: Issues in American Education* (New York: John Day, 1968), pp. 69-84.

11. R. E. Phillips, "To Placate the Angry," *Educational Leadership* (Feb. 1972), p. 436.

12. For the popularist point of view of this interpretation, see Vance Packard, *The Waste Makers* (New York: McKay, 1960). The complex leftist intellectual's view is given in Herbert Marcuse, *One-Dimensional Man* (Boston: Beacon, 1964). An unusually anti-establishment (but pro-educational) version designed for the front-line educator (classroom teacher, school administrator), sure to raise the hackles of those not yet inclined to react emotionally to social issues in their educational context, is George Henderson, ed., *Education for Peace: Focus on Mankind* (Washington D.C.: Association for Supervision and Curriculum Development, 1973).(The 1973 Yearbook of ASCD.)

13. J. K. Gailbraith, *The New Industrial State.* pp. 400-401.

14. Edward F. Denison, *Why Growth Rates Differ* (Washington, D.C.: The Brookings Institution, 1967).

15. Ibid., p. 78.

16. Ibid., pp. 105-6.

17. George Psacharopoulos, assisted by Keith Hinchliffe, *Returns to Education: an International Comparison* (San Francisco, Calif.: Jossey-Bass/Elsevier, 1972), chap. 5.

18. Ibid., chaps. 5, 6, 9.

19. See Chris Argyris, *Personality and Organization* (New York: Harper, 1957). See also Erich Fromm, *The Sane Society* (New York: Rinehart, 1955).

20. The term *technical barbarism* has been used by the educational sociologist Burton R. Clark. See his *Educating the Expert Society* (San Francisco, Calif.: Chandler, 1962), pp. 288 ff.

21. Galbraith, in his *The New Industrial State*, pp. 299-303, examines other and related aspects of this matter, dealing with the more general issues of how the scientific-educational "estate" adjusts its attitudes and behaviors to suit the industrial technostructure and, not strangely, vice versa.

22. Alvin Toffler, *Future Shock* (New York: Random House, 1970), p. 357.

23. Jencks, esp. pp. 52-83, 135-75, 253-65.

24. James S. Coleman, *Equality of Educational Opportunity* (Washington, D.C.: Office of Education, 1965).

25. Jacques-François Revel, *Without Marx or Jesus* (New York: Doubleday, 1971), p. 164.

26. Toffler, p. 160.

27. Colin M. Turnbull, *The Mountain People* (New York: Simon & Schuster, 1972).

28. National Commission for Cooperative Education, "Colleges, Universities and Community Colleges Offering Cooperative Education Programs," Pamphlet of the Commission, 52 Vanderbilt Ave., New York, N.Y., Nov. 1, 1971.

29. See Peter F. Drucker, *The Age of Discontinuity* (New York: Harper, 1969), chap. 1.

30. See Donald N. Michael, *The Next Generation* (New York: Random House, 1965), pp. 39 ff., 188-93.

Chapter 4

1. Friedrich Nietzsche, *On the Future of Our Educational Institutions* (New York: Macmillan, 1924).

2. See, among other writings of the author that bear on this point, Paul Woodring, *Introduction to American Education* (New York: Harcourt, Brace, 1965), pp. 48 ff.

3. For the reader who wishes to pursue further and in greater depth this issue of how bureaucratic systems and the professions function, in ways hidden to the average citizen, to maintain and develop in-group domination over certain classes of activity of social importance, the best recent work is Corrine L. Gilb, *Hidden Hierarchies* (New York: Harper, 1966).

4. Many sources, government and private, are available to the reader who wishes to follow the total employment-unemployment picture in the U.S. over the years. NEA (National Education Association) and the USOE (United States Office of Education) publish various reference bulletins indicationg the year-by-year supply-demand ratios for teachers and educational administrators. For a recent analysis of the down-trend in teacher hiring and its implications, consult Alfred Lightfoot, "Teacher Surplus in the Seventies: Educational and Sociological Implications," in A. Lightfoot, ed., *Inquiries Into the Social Foundations of Education* (Chicago: Rand McNally, 1972), pp. 357-63.

5. S. P. Marland, "The School's Role in Career Development," *Educational Leadership* (Dec. 1972), pp. 203-5.

6. A difficult but rewarding discussion of various historical and contemporary understandings of liberal or general education is contained in Paul H. Hirst, "Liberal Education and the Nature of Knowlege," in Cornelius J. Troost, ed., *Radical School Reform: Critique and Alternatives* (Boston: Little, Brown, 1973), pp. 91-114.

7. A. N. Whitehead, *The Aims of Education and Other Essays* (New York: Macmillan, 1929): p. 1.

8. Van Cleve Morris, *Philosophy and the American School* (Boston: Houghton Mifflin, 1961), p. 306.

9. See Lawrence Fedigan, "Conceptual Systems Theory and Teaching," *Educational Leadership* (May 1973), pp. 765-68.

10. See Robert F. Mager, *Preparing Objectives for Programmed Instruction* (San Francisco, Calif.: Fearon, 1962). See Also Robert M. Gagné, "Behavioral Objectives? Yes!" *Educational Leadership* (Feb. 1972), pp. 394-96.

11. Robert M. Gagné, *The Conditions of Learning* (New York: Holt, 1966), p. 242.

12. Ibid., p. 243.

13. A synoptic view of the major points of dispute on both sides is given in pro-and-con articles appearing in the February 1972 issue of *Educational Leadership*. See Gagné, "Behavioral Objectives? Yes!" and George F. Kneller, "Behavioral Objectives? No!", pp. 394-96, 397-400.

14. Kneller, "Behavioral Objectives? No!", p. 400.

15. Ibid., p. 397.

16. See Bruce R. Joyce, "Curriculum and Humanistic Education: 'Monolism' vs. 'Pluralism,' " in Carl Weinberg, ed., *Humanistic Foundations of Education* (Englewood Cliffs, N.J.: Prentice-Hall, 1972).

17. Lady Bridget Plowden, "Reflections and Projections Concerning Open Education." Address to the Forum of the New York State Education Department, May 1973. Reported by Mark Masterson, Education Section, *Christian Science Monitor*, June 12, 1973, p. 12.

18. Ibid.

19. See B. F. Skinner, "The Science of Learning and the Art of Teaching," *Harvard Educational Review* 24 (Spring 1954). See also B. F. Skinner, *The Technology of Teaching* (New York: Appleton, 1968).

20. See Gilbert Highet, *The Art of Teaching* (New York: Knopf, 1950), pp. 49-53.

21. That teacher inputs can make a significant difference and that this difference may depend in great part upon the various qualities (taken separately and in combination) that different teachers possess is strongly implied by a very dependable source, i.e., James S. Coleman, "Increasing Educational Opportunity," in S. M. McMurrin, ed., *The Conditions for Educational Equality* (New York: The Commission for Economic Development, 1971), pp. 104-21.

Chapter 5

1. John Dewey, *Democracy and Education* (New York: Macmillan, 1916), p. 338.

2. D. E. Berlyne, "Recent Developments in Piaget's Work," in R. C. Anderson and D. P. Ausubel, eds., *Readings in the Psychology of Cognition* (New York: Holt, 1965), pp. 173-93.

3. David Elkind, "What Does Piaget Say to the Teacher?", *Today's Education* (Nov. 1972), p. 48.

4. Jean Piaget and associates, *The Moral Judgment of the Child*, trans. Marjorie Gabain (London: Routledge and Kegan Paul, 1932), p. 407.

5. Ibid., p. 404

6. Ibid., p. 409

7. Ibid., p. 411

8. Ibid., p. 412

9. Mario Fantini, "Address to Wingspread Conference on Educational Alternatives," quoted in *Changing Schools, Original Newsletter on Alternative Schools*, no. 002, undated, Educational Alternatives Project, Indiana University/National Consortium of Alternative Schools, p. 3.

Chapter 6

1. Gagné, *The Conditions of Learning*, p. 5.

2. By far the most successful activator of this issue, with his contention (supported by a scholarly argument at great length) that genetic factors substantially prevent hoped-for success of compensatory education programs among disadvanced learners by virtue of their relatively absolute predetermination of an effective upper limit for learning, is Arthur R. Jensen. See his "How Much Can

We Boost I.Q. and Scholastic Achievement?", *Harvard Educational Review* 39, no. 1 (Winter 1969): 1-123.

3. Darwin, *Origin of Species*, 11:91.

4. W. L. Mallmann, "Health Hazards in Our Environment," in Donald A. Read, ed., *New Directions in Health Education* (New York: Macmillan, 1971), p. 205.

5. See Berton Roeche, *Eleven Blue Men* (Boston: Little, Brown, 1953).

6. Darwin, p. 42.

7. William Shockley, Address to Annual Meeting of the American Psychological Association. Washington D.C., Sept. 7, 1972. Reported in *Chicago Tribune*, Sept. 8, 1972.

8. Ibid.

9. Ibid.

10. Burton R. Clark, *Educating the Expert Society* (San Francisco, Calif.: Chandler, 1962).

11. Some of the conflicts posed by state involvement in matters of public interest, e.g., public health, regulation of services, aesthetic elements in the environment, education as a social necessity are aired in J. Kenneth Galbraith, *The New Industrial State* (Boston: Houghton Mifflin, 1967), chaps. 30-35.

12. Konrad Lorenz, *Evolution and Modification of Behavior* (Chicago: University of Chicago Press, 1965), p. 20.

13. Alain Touraine, *The Post-Industrial Society*, trans. L. F. X. Mayhew (New York: Random House, 1971), p. 225.

14. Peter F. Drucker, *The Age of Discontinuity* (New York: Harper, 1969), chap. 1.

15. Gagné, *The Conditions of Learning*.

16. B. F. Skinner, *The Technology of Teaching* (New York: Appleton-Century-Crofts, 1968).

17. David P. Ausubel, *Educational Psychology: A Cognitive View* (New York: Holt, 1968), chaps. 2 and 3.

18. Mark Terry, *Teaching for Survival* (New York: Friends of the Earth/Ballantine, 1971), pp. 10-17.

19. Ibid., pp. 47-193.

20. Barbara J. Kohuth and Boyd T. Marsh, "Environment in Education: A Pragmatic Look," *Educational Leadership* (April 1973), pp. 656-57.

21. The literature dealing with group effects on individual performance is extensive. Classic studies include the following, each tending to demonstrate how,

under different conditions, social influences determine how a large percentage of people under observation behave: K. Lewin, "Forces behind Food Habits and Methods of Change," *Bulletin of the National Research Council 108* (1943) 35-65; E. B. Bennett, "Discussion, Decision, Commitment, and Consensus in 'Group Decision,' " *Human Relations 8* (1955): 251-73; S. Milgram, "Group Pressure and Action against a Person," *Journal of Abnormal Social Psychology 69* (1964): 137-43.

22. Ford Foundation Task Force on Higher Education, Frank Newman, Chairman, *Report on Higher Education* (Washington, D.C.: U.S. Government Printing Office, March 1971).

23. John Dewey, *Democracy and Education* (New York: Macmillan, 1916).

24. See Peter T. White, "Behold the Computer Revolution." *National Geographic* (Nov. 1970), pp. 630 ff.

25. Ibid., p. 627.

26. Ibid.

Chapter 7

1. J. Edwin Becht, *A Geography of Transportation and Business Logistics* (Dubuque, Iowa: W. C. Brown, 1970), p. 63.

2. See Peter F. Drucker, *The Age of Discontinuity* (New York: Harper, 1969), chap. 1.

3. David K. Cohen and Marvin Lazerson, "Education and the Corporate Order," *Socialist Revolution* (March/April 1972), p. 72.

4. See Boyd Keenan, "The Energy Crisis and Its Meaning for American Culture," *The Christian Century*, July 18-25, 1973, pp. 756-59.

5. Ibid., p. 759.

6. See Bayard Rustin, "The Mind of the Black Militant," in Alvin Toffler, ed., *The Schoolhouse in the City* (New York: Praeger, 1968), pp. 34-35.

7. See especially Bruce R. Joyce, "Curriculum and Humanistic Education: 'Monolism' vs. 'Pluralism'," in Carl Weinberg, ed., *Humanistic Foundations of Education* (Englewood Cliffs, N.J.: Prentice-Hall, 1972). See also Urie Bronfenbrenner, *Two Worlds of Childhood — USA and USSR* (New York: Russell Sage Foundation, 1970), esp. chap. 6.

8. Loren Eiseley, *The Mind as Nature* (New York: Harper and Row, 1962), p. 52.

Bibliography

Books

Argyris, Chris. *Personality and Organization.* New York: Harper, 1957.

Ausubel, David P. *Educational Psychology: A Cognitive View.* New York: Holt, 1968.

Becht, J. Edwin. *A Geography of Transportation and Business Logistics.* Dubuque, Iowa: W.C. Brown, 1970.

Bronfenbrenner, Urie. *Two Worlds of Childhood — USA and USSR.* New York: Russell Sage Foundation, 1970.

Clark, Burton R. *Educating the Expert Society.* San Francisco: Chandler, 1962.

Coleman, James S. *Equality of Educational Opportunity.* Washington, D.C.: Office of Education, 1965.

Darwin, Charles. *Origin of Species.* Harvard Classics Edition, vol. 11. New York: Collier, 1937.

Denison, Edward F. *Why Growth Rates Differ.* Washington, D.C.: The Brookings Institution, 1967.

Dewey, John. *Democracy and Education.* New York: Macmillan, 1916.

Drucker, Peter F. *The Age of Discontinuity.* New York: Harper, 1969.

235

Du Nouÿ, Pierre L. *Human Destiny.* New York: Longmans, Green, 1947.

Eells, Kenneth, et. al. *Intelligence and Cultural Differences: A Study of Cultural Learning and Problem Solving.* Chicago: University of Chicago Press, 1951.

Eiseley, Loren. *The Mind as Nature.* New York: Harper, 1962.

Fromm, Erich. *The Sane Society.* New York: Rinehart, 1955.

Gagné, Robert M. *The Conditions of Learning.* New York: Holt, 1966.

Galbraith, J. Kenneth. *The Affluent Society.* Boston: Houghton Mifflin, 1958.

————*The New Industrial State.* New York: New American Library, 1967.

Gilb, Corrine L. *Hidden Hierarchies.* New York: Harper, 1966.

Goble, Frank G. *The Third Force — The Psychology of Abraham Maslow.* New York: Grossman/Viking, 1970.

Greer, Colin. *The Great School Legend: A Revisionist Interpretation of American Public Education.* New York: Basic Books, 1972.

Henderson, George, ed. *Education for Peace: Focus on Mankind.* Washington, D.C.: Association for Supervision and Curriculum Development, 1973. (The Yearbook of ASCD).

Highet, Gilbert. *The Art of Teaching.* New York: Knopf, 1950.

Hoffer, Eric. *The True Believer.* New York: Harper, 1951.

Jencks, Christopher. *Inequality: A Reassessment of the Effect of Family and Schooling in America.* New York: Basic Books, 1972.

Lightfoot, Alfred, ed. *Inquiries into the Social Foundations of Education.* Chicago: Rand McNally, 1972.

Lorenz, Konrad. *Evolution and Modification of Behavior.* Chicago: University of Chicago Press, 1965.

McMurrin, S. M., ed. *The Conditions for Educational Equality.* New York: The Commission for Economic Development, 1971.

Mager, Robert F. *Preparing Objectives for Programmed Instruction.* San Francisco: Fearon, 1962.

Marcuse, Herbert. *One-Dimensional Man.* Boston: Beacon, 1964.

Maslow, Abraham H. *Motivation and Personality.* New York: Harper, 1954.

Michael, Donald. *The Next Generation.* New York: Random House, 1965.

Morris, Van Cleve. *Philosophy and the American School.* Boston: Houghton Mifflin, 1961.

Newman, Frank, Chairman, Ford Foundation Task Force on Higher Education. *Report on Higher Education.* Washington: U.S. Government Printing Office, 1971.

Nietzche, Friedrich. *On the Future of Our Educational Institutions.* New York: Macmillan, 1924.

————*The Use and Abuse of History.* Translated by Adrian Collins. New York and Indianapolis: Bobbs-Merrill, 1957.

Packard, Vance. *Nation of Strangers.* New York: McKay, 1972.

————*The Waste Makers.* New York: McKay, 1960.

Piaget, Jean, and Associates. *The Moral Judgement of the Child.* Translated by Marjorie Gabain. London: Routledge and Kegan Paul, 1932.

Psacharopoulos, George, assisted by Keith Hinchcliffe. *Returns to Education: an International Comparison.* San Francisco: Jossey-Bass/Elsevier, 1972.

Read, Donald A., ed. *New Directions in Health Education.* New York: Macmillan, 1971.

Revel, Jacques-François. *Without Marx or Jesus.* New York: Doubleday, 1971.

Roeche, Berton. *Eleven Blue Men.* Boston: Little, Brown, 1953.

Skinner, B. F. *The Technology of Teaching.* New York: Appleton, 1968.

Solzhenitsyn, Alexander. *Nobel Lecture.* Translated by F. D. Reeve. New York: Farrar, Straus & Giroux, 1972.

Terry, Mark. *Teaching for Survival.* New York: Friends of the Earth/Ballantine, 1971.

Toffler, Alvin. *Future Shock.* New York: Random House, 1970.

Touraine, Alain. *The Post-Industrial Society.* New York: Random House, 1971.

Troost, Cornelius, ed. *Radical School Reform: Critique and Alternatives.* Boston: Little, Brown, 1973.

Trunbull, Colin. *The Mountain People.* New York: Simon and Schuster, 1972.

Weinberg, Carl, ed. *Humanistic Foundations of Education.* Englewood Cliffs, N.J.: Prentice Hall, 1972.

Whitehead, Alfred N. *The Aims of Education and Other Essays.* New York: Macmillan, 1929.

Woodring, Paul. *Introduction to American Education.* New York: Harcourt, Brace, 1965.

Periodical Literature

Bennett, E. B. "Discussion, Decision, Commitment, and Consensus in 'Group Decision.' " *Human Relations* 8 (1955): 251-73.

Berlyne, D. E. "Recent Developments in Piaget's Work." Reprinted in R. C. Anderson and D. P. Ausubel, eds. *Readings in the Psychology of Cognition.* New York: Holt, 1965.

Cohen, David K., and Lazerson, Marvin. "Education and the Corporate Order." *Socialist Revolution* (March/April 1972).

Comstock, R. W. "Man and His Environment: One Industrial Point of View." *The Science Teacher* 37, no. 6 (September 1970).

Doll, Ronald C. "Alternative Forms of Schooling." *Educational Leadership* 29, no. 5 (February 1972).

Elkind, David. "What Does Piaget Say to the Teacher?" *Today's Education* (November 1972).

Fantini, Mario. "Address to Wingspread Conference on Educational Alternatives." *Changing Schools, Original Newsletter on Alternative Schools,* no. 002 (n.d.). Indiana University/National Consortium of Alternative Schools.

Fedigan, Lawrence. "Conceptual Systems Theory and Teaching." *Educational Leadership* (May 1972).

"Fighting to Save the Earth from Man." *Time Magazine,* February 2, 1970.

Gagné, Robert M. "Behavioral Objectives? Yes!" *Educational Leadership* (February 1972).

Hardin, Garrett. "The Tragedy of the Commons." *Science,* December 13, 1968. (Reprinted in Mary E. Hawkins, ed., *Vital Views of the Environment.* Washington, D. C.: National Science Teachers Assocation, 1970.)

Jensen, Arthur R. "How Much Can We Boost I.Q. and Scholastic Achievement?" *Harvard Educational Review* 39, no. 1 (Winter 1969).

Keenan, Boyd. "The Energy Crisis and Its Meaning for American Culture." *The Christian Century*, July 18-25, 1973.

Kneller, George F. "Behavioral Objectives? No!" *Educational Leadership* (February 1972).

Kohuth, Barbara, and Marsh, Boyd T. "Environment in Education: A Pragmatic Look." *Educational Leadership* (April 1973).

Lewin, Kurt. "Forces Behind Food Habits and Methods of Change." *Bulletin of the National Research Council* 108 (1943): 35-65.

Marland, S. P. "The School's Role in Career Development." *Educational Leadership* (December 1972).

Milgram, S. "Group Pressure and Action Against a Person." *Journal of Abnormal Social Psychology* 69 (1964): 137-43.

Mitroff, I. I., and Betz, Frederick. "Dialectical Decision Theory: A Meta-Theory of Decision-Making." *Management Science* 19, no. 1. (September 1972).

National Commission for Cooperative Education. "Colleges, Universities and Community Colleges Offering Cooperative Education Programs," Pamphlet Series of the Commission, November 1, 1971.

Phillips, Romeo E. "To Placate the Angry." *Educational Leadership* (February 1972).

Plowden, Lady Bridget. "Reflections and Projections Concerning Open Education." Address to the Forum of the New York State Education Department, May 1973. Reported by Mark Masterson, Education Section, *Christian Science Monitor*, June 12, 1973.

Rustin, Bayard. "The Mind of the Black Militant." Reprinted in Alvin Toffler, ed. *The Schoolhouse in the City*. New York: Praeger, 1968.

Shockley, William. Address to Annual Meeting of the American Psychological Association. Washington, D.C., September 7, 1972. Reported in *Chicago Tribune*, September 8, 1972.

Skinner, B. F. "The Science of Learning and the Art of Teaching." *Harvard Educational Review* 24 (Spring 1954).

Stillman, Calvin W. "Reflections on Environmental Education." *Teachers College Record* 74, no. 2 (December 1972).

White, Peter T. "Behold the Computer Revolution." *National Geographic* (November 1970).

Index

241

See also Behavior; Communications revolution; Corporations; Environmental learning; Individual; Learning; Masses; Mass media; Reinvestment; Self-development; Social management; Social environment

Adult work environment, transformation of, 85-86. *See also* Corporations; Communications revolution

Adversary approach to energy problem, 204-5

Advertising, 37-38. *See also* Communications revolution

Aerospace industry, 89

Affective component of environmental education, 218-20

Affective powers of individual, 218-19

Affective states, importance of in reactions to stimuli, 118-19. *See also* Conditioning; Conditioned learning; Traditional learning

Affluence: theoretical inevitability of, 159-60; uncertain as base for social planning, 139-40. *See also* Abundance; Consumer

Age of Anxiety, The, 223

Age-appropriateness of environmental education, 167-68

Aggression in children, 149

Allende, Salvador, 194

America, model of capitalist society, 50-51

Anderson, R. C., 119n, 232

Anterior needs. *See* Maslow, Abraham

Anti-environmental behaviors, 157-58. *See also* Adaptation; Adapted person

Argyris, Chris, 62, 229, 235

Assembly line, as requiring alternative educational measures, 63-64

AT&T Corporation, telecommunications systems of, 83

Attitude, teachers', open, 109

Attitude change, mass, 36-37. *See also*

Adult education; Conditioned learning; Education, mass; Environmental general education; Environmental learning

Ausubel, David P., 119n, 154, 232, 233, 235

Authority, shared, in corporate structure, 84

Automobile manufacturers, 59-60

Awareness, individual, and new education, 161. *See also* Conditioned learning; Counter-learning

Background experience, nonacademic, of "new" teacher, 110

Balance: as environmental necessity, 29-30; in environmental teaching, 114; natural, human interference in, 9. *See also* Environmental general education; Environmental learning

Balance-point, individual, and environmental learning, 219-20

Becht, J. Edwin, quoted 192, 234, 235

Behavior: adjustment, 8-9; as block to social equity, 149-50; conditioning of, 154-56; consistent performances of, 154; coping, 190; criteria of judgement of, 23-24; direction of, in "school of tomorrow," 182-85; environmental shaping of through education, 111; as evidence of learning, 138; futurist, development of, 84-85; human, and dominance, 10; management of, 196-98; directed, 160-61, 199; predictability of, 154-55; and self-development, 198-99; socially conditioned, 158-59; two stages in management of, 197-98. *See also* Adaptation; Affective states; Communications industry; Communications revolution; Conflict; Conditioning; Counter-conditioning; Cybernations; Cybernetics;